A Nondualistic
Pentecostal Theology

A Nondualistic Pentecostal Theology

Exploring Dialectics and Becoming through Amos Yong and Slavoj Žižek

Spencer Moffatt

LEXINGTON BOOKS/FORTRESS ACADEMIC
Lanham • Boulder • New York • London

Published by Lexington Books/Fortress Academic
Lexington Books is an imprint of The Rowman & Littlefield Publishing Group, Inc.
4501 Forbes Boulevard, Suite 200, Lanham, Maryland 20706
www.rowman.com

86-90 Paul Street, London EC2A 4NE

Copyright © 2025 by The Rowman & Littlefield Publishing Group, Inc.

Excerpt from *The Spirit Poured Out on All Flesh* by Amos Yong, copyright © 2005.
Used by permission of Baker Academic, a division of Baker Publishing Group.

All rights reserved. No part of this book may be reproduced in any form or by any
electronic or mechanical means, including information storage and retrieval systems,
without written permission from the publisher, except by a reviewer who may quote
passages in a review.

British Library Cataloguing in Publication Information Available

Library of Congress Cataloging-in-Publication Data Available

ISBN 978-1-9787-1056-6 (cloth : alk. paper)
ISBN 978-1-9787-1057-3 (electronic)

♾™ The paper used in this publication meets the minimum requirements of American
National Standard for Information Sciences—Permanence of Paper for Printed Library
Materials, ANSI/NISO Z39.48-1992.

Contents

Acknowledgments		vii
Introduction: From Dualism to Nondualism		1
1	Tracing the Groundwork	17
2	Amos Yong on Trinity, Dialectics, and Transcendence	37
3	Žižek's Hegelian Dialectics	55
4	Žižek on Transcendence and Trinity vis-à-vis Dialectics	81
5	A Speculative Modification of Amos Yong's Trinity, Dialectics, and Transcendence	97
6	God the Negative	119
Bibliography		135
Index		143
About the Author		147

v

Acknowledgments

I am convinced, now more than ever, that the intellectual journey is a combined endeavor. To those who have gone before me, I glean in the wake of your curiosity. To those who are beside me, your love has carried me through. To those who will come after me, go forth in courage.

Introduction

From Dualism to Nondualism

CLAIM

The trinitarian and dialectical contours of Amos Yong's theology warrant the intervention of Žižek's Hegelian dialectics to resolve the incoherence between philosophical and theological claims. Namely, between (1) a non-substance metaphysic (i.e., critical metaphysic[1]), relational ontology, and dialectical methodology and (2) a substance metaphysic (i.e., classical metaphysic),[2] fixed divine subjectivity, and dualistic/non-speculative transcendence (i.e., transcendence as external to the world). In short, whereas Yong's philosophical claims are pointed toward the speculative aspect of the dialectic, his theological claims are grounded in a classical metaphysic, revealing the location of dissonance.

In resolve, Yong's theology is revised to establish a coherent relationship with his philosophy and, along the way, reconcile the dichotomous use of (1) non-substance or substance, (2) relational or non-relational, (3) dialectical or non-dialectical, and (4) speculative or non-speculative, depending upon the type of context or claim involved. Put differently, reconciliation consists of the sublative movement from the latter to the former of each set.

Žižek implicitly addresses such problems with his *demonstration* of the speculative, for he understands his work as practicing, not presenting, dialectics.[3] As Žižek explains, "we should read the term 'dialectics' in the Greek sense of *dialektika* (like *semeiotika* or *politika*): not as a universal notion, but as 'dialectical [semiotic, political] matters', as an inconsistent (non-All) mixture."[4] Meaning, dialectics is not a "universal notion" or isolated method to be coldly applied to specific situations; rather, it is a way of conceptualizing the world with the realization that everything is already a non-universal, non-isolated event. Thus, it is important to understand dialectics as indicative

1

of ontological incompletion and reflection thereof. Fredric Jameson makes a similar point about dialectics not being a sterile "system" or "method."[5] And Andrew Douglas sees dialectics as theoretical reflection upon the human experience of being "mired in the struggle."[6] The payoff is a Christian philosophical theology that maintains systematic coherence wherein divine subjectivity emerges through archaeology and teleology[7] with transcendence as the inherent dynamism of the self-overcoming dialectic amidst concrete particularity. In short, God shapes, and is shaped by, the World.

Slavoj Žižek is thus the catalyst of choice for the critical extension of Yong's theological claims into philosophical alignment. In this vein, Žižek exemplifies the process of allowing one's claims to go "to their end"[8] thereby opening one's assumptions to dialectical critique within the overall transition from the classical to the critical.[9] The result is a speculative theology that consists of a relational ontology, complex substance, and dialectical rhythm that sustains a logic capable of immanentizing Yong's trinity, dialectic, and transcendence. In other words, reinscribing the external remainders that exist within Yong's theology, for example, God as existing in a supernatural—versus natural—dimension, into a philosophical theology that is ontologically complex and relational. As a result, for example, the traditional separation of the immanent from the economic (in trinitarian theology) is discerned to be a dualistic projection. Žižek's commitment to the speculative mode of the dialectic impacts Yong's theology insofar as the conceptual and paradigmatic transformation of his theology opens the reality of human/finite participation in the actualization of divine/infinite subjectivity akin to a *communicatio idiomatum* of the (non-)Whole. It is here, in the speculative mode of dialectics, that the theologian can reasonably posit God as being relational.

For the sake of clarity, my working definition of metaphysics is the relational constellation of Thought, Language, Being, and Reality. Within that, *substance* metaphysics has to do with a metaphysic that consists of Being as a static substance that exists on its own regardless of accidents, contingencies, and predications. For example, in Christian theology, the possibility of perpetuating a (classical) substance metaphysic is attached to the way(s) in which the documents and creeds of the early ecumenical councils are interpreted and disseminated. Contemporary interpretations of the various concepts and categories used to specify the divine nature of the trinity are best interpreted retroactively rather than proactively. This means that contemporary understandings of what the divine nature consists of are critically retrieved, not read forward. Therefore, a definitive understanding of divine nature is not bound to the particularities of ancient confessions such as Nicaea, Constantinople, or Chalcedon. While these councils are necessarily taken into consideration given their historical importance, their metaphysical paradigms are critically engaged in the third millennium.

Introduction 3

In contrast, *speculative* metaphysics is the combination of determinate (finite) and *in*determinate (infinite) modes of existence. While inheriting the substance version of metaphysics, speculative metaphysics goes beyond such by welcoming the transcendent quality of being insofar as the finite and the infinite are inextricable within a non-substance metaphysic. The speculative, therefore, sublates the reductive claims of (1) *subjective determination* in modern empiricism's claim that truth must be empirically proven and (2) *objective indetermination* in the sense of Truth as ultimately inaccessible. Speculative metaphysics thus works itself out through a dialectical approach insofar as the concepts used by Thought to make sense of Being are involved in its actualization. Hence, according to Alain Badiou, "metaphysics demands the courage of thought."[10]

To reiterate, though, dialectics is not an abstract method to be applied at will as if form were separate from content.[11] It is an impression of the relationality and rationality of all categories and concepts involved in the movement of Thought and Being within Becoming.[12] The speculative dialectic, then, is not driven by a thing but by nothing/negativity, thus able to disrupt discrete formalizations of categories and concepts, releasing them back into their native environment of the liminal space between possibility and actuality, that is, amidst the evolution of the concept (*Begriff*). All of which emphasizes the always available space of potential. The creativity of the negative is thus a doubling, the reflexive capacity of the negative to create change in position and perspective, which enacts the positive impact of negativity.[13] Speculative Reason (*Vernunft*) thus manifests in and through the actuality of being, thereby refuting the one-sidedness of subjective finitude and/or objective infinitude insofar as the finite and the infinite are simultaneous dynamics in relationality. The speculative version of dialectics, then, involves "the whole terrain of thought."[14]

Honing in, the creativity of negativity is observed in its doubling, that is, in its reflexive capacity, that creates a parallax shift, or a change in perspective, wherein negativity is kinetic to life.[15] Indeed, for Hegel, negativity is "the principle of all self-movement," shattering impositions of stasis.[16] This speculative capacity of negativity is garnered by Žižek's dialectical materialism when he writes that "the axiom of true materialism is not 'material reality is all there is', but a double one: (1) there is nothing which is not material reality, (2) material reality is non-All."[17] The non-All signals the non-reductive description of materialism wherein the Hegelian negative breaks out of reified empiricism, positivism, and/or idealism. A speculative metaphysic thus integrates the dialectical impacts of the material upon the immaterial and vice versa. Meaning, objectivity is established in the approach of the subjective thus highlighting the importance of Kant's transcendental critique within Hegel's philosophy of Spirit.[18] Otherwise,

4   *Introduction*

"we regress to the standard metaphysical notion of Truth as a substantial In-Itself, independent of the subject's approach to it."[19] Žižek's dialectical materialism is therefore a speculative movement based upon Hegel's "tarrying with the negative" that includes the deconstructive and constructive capacities. Lastly, my use of "network" throughout signifies the becoming aspect of being and reality in a conceptual model premised upon the priority of change and development over and against stasis and stagnancy. There is nothing outside of the network because all things are immanent and realized as products of dynamic processes and events, thus disclosing the emerging state of a network.[20]

PROVOCATION

Throughout his work, Yong proclaims that philosophy has "moved away from the substance-accident metaphysics of Aristotelianism."[21] That "substance metaphysics has long since given way to a variety of process-oriented and relational metaphysics, along with their attending theologies."[22] That a rigorous theology is one that is "outside of a substance metaphysics"[23] insofar as "[b]elievers encounter the living Christ who is present, understood not in the physicalist or consubstantive terms of Aristotelian and neoscholastic substance philosophy but in the interpersonal and intersubjective terms of contemporary pneumatological theology."[24] That "it is a mistake to think of God as a subject in Cartesian and modern individualistic categories."[25] That "it is a mistake to think of God as a subject in Cartesian and modern individualistic categories."[26] He goes so far as to critique the interpretation of patristic theology as being driven by a classical substance metaphysic. As Yong writes, "the unintentional elevation to dogma of the metaphysics of substance undergirding the patristic creeds when in point of fact, the Church Fathers were motivated primarily by soteriological rather than by metaphysical concerns."[27] Historically necessary, sure, but the metaphysical paradigms of antiquity continue to be confronted with, and reinterpreted by, critique. Hence, the interpretations of the concepts and categories used to specify the divine nature of the trinity remain open to ongoing retrieval and reinterpretation insofar as "Truth itself coincides with the path towards Truth."[28]

Yong consistently argues that a philosophical "breakthrough" occurs with "the paradigmatic transition from the Aristotelian substance ontology to the Einsteinian universe," wherein "relations" and "participation" take precedence.[29] That "an ontology of becoming" emerges from the ruins of a "classical ontology of being."[30] Therefore, this paradigmatic shift in metaphysics and ontology is one that has "bypassed the essentialisms (chiefly, the Platonic ideas and the Aristotelian substance)."[31] It is a movement beyond "Plato's

Introduction 5

dualism [which] promoted a static worldview" and "Aristotle's substance metaphysics" that "could not account for genuinely changing things."[32]

In praising the metaphysical contributions of Charles Sanders Peirce, Yong writes:

[Peirce] overcomes all of the dualisms of the philosophical tradition. Plato's unchanging ideas and changing phenomena, for example, undergird other misleading notions, such as the gnostic devaluation of the material world and the Kantian *noumena-phenomena* dualism. Whereas Peirce's categories of Firstness and Secondness account for Plato's ideas and phenomena, Thirdness means that reality is dynamic, always becoming something else, as its laws and habits mediate the transformation of the present into the future. Similarly, the Cartesian mind-body problematic, imbued as it is with medieval nominalism, is resolved in a triadic metaphysics that defines nature's processes in semiotic terms, on the one hand, and sees human cognition as a higher-level manifestation of the category of law, on the other. Finally, Aristotelian substance dualism is replaced with a dynamic view of reality shaped by real laws and habits. Essentialism, the idea that things have definite and immutable identities, is rejected insofar as essences become the hows of experience (qualities that make things present to us, which we then reify and arrange alphabetically in dictionaries), which are continuously evolving according to their accumulation of habits and tendencies, rather than whats (facts that resist or oppose us).[33]

Despite all this rigorous movement toward nondualism, his language—in particular, theological language—periodically resorts to dualism. As a standard of judgment, Yong claims that if a theologian adheres to the proposition that God is *not* "dependent upon the world," that is, that God "transcends this world," then one is a proponent of "theological dualism."[34] Based upon this standard, his endorsement of divine action as "unilateral" implies theological dualism.[35] Given the statement that he does "*not* hold that God as spirit is . . . an emergent reality like human spirits" is also indicative of dualism.[36] With his contemporary endorsement of the classical understanding of *creatio ex nihilo*, "the complete dependence of the world on such a transcendent source," and the "radically other[ness]" of God, again, suggestive of theological dualism.[37]

This oscillation between nondualism and dualism makes more sense with the realization that Yong's philosophy leans nondualist whereas his theology leans dualist, that is, his philosophy prefers non-substance conceptualization whereas his theology prefers substance conceptualization. One can see the tension that exists between these two thrusts in the following section:

How do we avoid favoring being to the neglect of becoming or vice-versa? What about substance and process; idealism and realism; universality and

6   *Introduction*

particularity; eternity and time; infinitude and finitude; possibility and actuality; the question of the one and the many? Is it truly the case that metaphysically, one of each side of these two polarities is more "true" to the way things are? Even if so, how do we know so? My own response is that whatever the truth to these metaphysical questions, the verdict is still out. Let the inquiry continue.[38]

My response to this oscillation is a commitment to nondualism, thereby critically updating theological claims for coherence with his philosophical claims.

In the most sustained and comprehensive analysis of Amos Yong's philosophical and theological methods, Pentecostal theologian Christopher Stephenson raises the following core problem:

> [Yong] assumes at a number of places that a metaphysic predicated on the category of substance is no longer tenable in a postmodern world. Nevertheless, he continues to trade on theological categories such as intra-trinitarian processions, *filioque*, and *perichoresis*, which are imbedded in a substance metaphysics.[39]

Stephenson is not discounting Yong's work; rather, he is pointing out the dissonance between Yong's (1) *critical* logic that undergirds his philosophical claims and (2) *classical* logic that undergirds his theological claims.[40] Stephenson goes on to suggest that "additional consideration of its viability [i.e., viability of Yong's trinitarian theology] within the context of a relational metaphysic could prove to be a fruitful line of inquiry for both Yong and his critics."[41]

The problem, as it turns out, is not Yong's use of classically defined theological concepts per se, but *as is*; that is to say, theological concepts without critical reconceptualization. The categories and concepts that Yong uses to communicate trinitarian identity, subjectivity, and relationality have not yet been translated into a complex metaphysic and non-substance relational ontology wherein divine subjectivity is dialectically anchored in interrelational events.[42]

While Yong does posit a relational ontology regarding human subjectivity, he does not go to the dialectical end, as it were, and include divine subjectivity in the mix. Yong's doctrine of God remains, by default, theoretically bound to classical theism and its divine personalism, wherein God is conceived of as an isolated subject/being that exists external to the world, thereby retaining the problem of dualism—understood here as transcendence over and against immanence—in his God-World relationality. This is a serious problem to be addressed in light of Yong's efforts to construct a "theological nondualism whereby God is neither merely immanent nor merely transcendent on the one hand, and neither merely emergent nor merely purposive and personal on the other."[43] Here, one can see the speculative potential within Yong's philosophical claims through his use of a dialectical *neither-nor* language, whereas

Introduction 7

his theological language tends to opt for dualistic *this-that* language, that is, God is this and creation is that.

The warrant for further critical analysis and engagement with the relation of theology and philosophy within Yong's overarching project is bolstered by his occasional looseness of argumentation. As L. William Oliverio notes in his review article of Yong's most in-depth methodological text, *Spirit-Word-Community*:

> [S]ometimes this project seems to suffer from vagueness. Some of this may be caused by the difficulty for the reader to keep up with the manifold correlations that he is making. But at other times it appears to be the result of the conflation of concepts under the use of a common term. . . . And at others he brings aspects of so many visions together that it seems that he should have offered more analytical clarity along the way. . . . Perhaps a future work could return to some of these issues in hermeneutics, epistemology, metaphysics or Trinity. Or a revised edition might offer some more clarity.[44]

This book, then, is a response to the combined critiques and corollary calls that are raised by Stephenson and Oliverio. To this end, I deal systematically, critically, and constructively with three interrelated motifs that make up the core of Yong's project: trinity, dialectic, and transcendence, given his statement that "any truly relational theology is necessarily *trinitarian*" and "robustly *dialectical*," that is, "dialectical."[45] All of which fund the "theological knowledge" of the "God-self-world" network.[46] In short, the task at hand is to flesh out the precision and coherence of Yong's theological argument that consists of the interrelation of trinity, dialectic, and transcendence.

THEOLOGICAL IMPETUS

Disconnections between philosophy and theology are typically caused by dialectical insufficiency, cropping up in Yong's systematic theology wherein philosophical claims and concepts are stopped short of their full impact upon theological claims and concepts. When conflicts between them arise, traditional theology retains its status as the ordering principle in relation to the whole and dialectical movement ceases. This problem manifests across theology in two paradigmatic ways: One, the theologian defaults to theological confession and ultimately relies upon a *reductio ad mysterium*, disclosing the false premise that faith and knowledge are two discrete categories that can be separated and ordered in hierarchical fashion with (traditional) faith reigning over (critical) knowledge.[47] This move hinges upon a belief in the "necessity of some kind of stable forms" and the dismissal of change and the evolutionary state of existence.[48] When faith is grounded in mystery and

8   *Introduction*

described as an act that precedes knowledge, classical doctrines of God are preserved with God being the perfect transcendent cause of an imperfect immanent world,[49] thus placing God outside of time and space.[50] Two, the theologian endorses a contemporary quantum ontology wherein matter is no longer conceptualized as a fixed substance responsible for linear causation[51] but as relational and evental amidst a complex and interconnected dynamism.[52] However, the theologian falls back upon the identification of God as a fixed substance externally positioned against the world evidenced by the use of theological concepts such as divine transcendence, sovereignty, providence, agency, impassibility, and immutability without critical comment and/or modification. Thus, the theologian ends up performing dissonance between a critical metaphysic and a substance metaphysic. In short, dialectical insufficiency reveals the non-dialectical relation of philosophy and theology by way of a theological confession wherein relationality is overridden by the "*irreducibl[e]* otherness of God" and the fundamental presence of an absolute difference that promotes the residual dualism of transcendence and immanence in the configuration of God and World.[53]

I contend that dialectical insufficiency and the retention of classical theological concepts are a result of theological creation (i.e., *arche*) and eschatological consummation (i.e., *telos*) as non-dialectical (i.e., one-sided, diachronic) events, therefore creating theological dependence upon an external agency that resists the dialectical modifications of complexity and plasticity.[54] God, separate from historical and dialectical participation, is thus assumed to be some*thing* that breaks *in* from some*where*, conceived as externally responsible for creation, consummation, and the terminable sustainability therein. The problem of dialectical insufficiency, then, presents with theological reliance upon the irreducible position of God as external— even when it is claimed that God is internally external—and theological one-sidedness that defaults to tradition, thereby articulating confessions of faith in a way that resists modification, evidenced by separations of God from World, theology from philosophy, and faith from knowledge.

STRUCTURE

My argument includes three interrelated parts: part I is analytical (chapters 1 and 2); part II is critical (chapters 3 and 4); and part III is constructive (chapters 5 and 6). Part I is the systematic analysis of Yong's trinity, dialectic, and transcendence vis-à-vis the God-World relation. The theological modules addressed in this section are Yong's foundational pneumatology, trialectical spiral, and pneumatological imagination insofar as they constitute and describe the conceptual movement within his systematic theology. I am particularly interested in his dialectics as the trialectical spiral, which consists of six sources of influence: scripture, theology, philosophy, metaphysics, epistemology, and hermeneutics. Insofar as the sublime object of theology is the God-World relationship, as Yong rightfully insists, the concept of transcendence is tracked down and reconfigured in dialectical becoming.[55]

Part II is the development of a critical theoretical framework via Slavoj Žižek in parallel to the three motifs in part I—trinity, dialectic, and transcendence—in preparation for part III's constructive modification of part I. I use Žižek's Hegelian dialectics for four reasons: First, Žižek's interpretations of Hegel indirectly respond to Yong's critiques of Hegel. Second, Žižek's Hegelian speculative dialectic provides the means necessary for tapping into the inherent speculative potential of Yong's philosophical claims. Third, Žižek brings with him the theological fruits of the Hegelian tradition insofar as he deals with the philosophical conceptualizations of trinity, dialectic, and transcendence. Fourth, Žižek's dialectical materialism provides the ontological texture of a speculative dialectic to be used by a constructive systematic theology that sublates classical theism's oppositional dyadic framework of God and World without doing away with divine uniqueness and mystery via Yong.

Hence, part III is the explicit return to Yong in light of Žižek's heuristic critique, thus allowing a constructive event to occur between the two approaches to trinity, dialectic, and transcendence. As a result, Yong's philosophical claims are committed to and radicalized, thereby internally modifying his own theological categories, concepts, and conclusions. The significant shift herein is the move from a classical understanding of transcendence to a speculative true infinite wherein God is not an object but a relational subject that is no longer beholden to the modern understanding of personhood. This means that subjectivity is no longer beholden to the presupposition of the classical understanding of divine Being as a predetermined, isolated subject that exists in-itself regardless of predication. Becoming is thus located prior to Being insofar as relationality, complexity, and plasticity undergird the God-World relation.[56]

This project is therefore a demonstration of the inherent capacity of Yong's philosophical claims to aid in the critical extension of his theological assertions, thereby sublating transcendence as something external to the world. For instance, Yong writes:

> The Spirit's reality is mediated through the particularly embodied experiences of the community of saints. There is therefore a unique sort of pentecostal sacramentality at work, an experiential and incarnational logic that acknowledges the Spirit's being made present and active through the materiality of personal embodiment and congregational life.[57]

10   *Introduction*

A speculative reading of Yong's claim that "the Spirit's being [is] made present and active through the materiality of personal embodiment and congregational life" means that the Spirit's being is not simply "mediated" by persons and communities but dialectically related to the "materiality of personal embodiment and congregational life." The "Spirit's being" is, therefore, necessarily "made present and active" in and through the speculative dialectic that is at work in the World. The *dynamism* of the speculative (i.e., dialectically relational) whole is thus understood as Hegel's *Geist* which ontologically emerges/ex-sists through the dialectic of the Whole.

NOTES

1. I plan on using "non-substance," "critical," and "speculative" interchangeably as representative of the aim of Amos Yong and the contribution of Slavoj Žižek. As Joseph Carew writes on Slavoj Žižek: "What thus makes Žižek's speculative real-idealism/ideal-realism . . . so penetrating and deserving of attention today is its ability to combine a profoundly idealist epistemology with a dynamic realist metaphysics in one single gesture, which shows us one path that contemporary metaphysics could take: namely, a *critical* one." Joseph Carew, *Ontological Catastrophe: Žižek and the Paradoxical Metaphysics of German Idealism* (Ann Arbor, MI: Open Humanities Press, 2014), 273.

2. Viz., trinitarian persons defined by substance metaphysics wherein a person is understood as an isolated, existing object of consciousness. Here I am borrowing and paraphrasing John Milbank's critique of Wolfhart Pannenberg's trinitarian theology which he identifies as a "trinitarian logic of substantial relations." Not that I agree with Milbank's critique or am correlating Yong to Pannenberg; rather, I simply like the phrasing of the particular idea of "substantial logic of trinitarian theology." The resolution would be to transition from a *substance logic* to a *speculative dialectical logic*. John Milbank, "The Second Difference: For a Trinitarianism without Reserve," *Modern Theology* 2:3 (1986): 213.

3. It is this speculative mode of the dialectic that Žižek identifies as one of Hegel's greatest contributions. "On a first approach (according to the official *doxa*), Hegel's thought is the ultimate example of the One overcoming its self-division through the Three (the 'synthesis' by means of which the One re-appropriates its alienated Otherness). It is thus true 'Hegel proposes a position of the three which is necessarily engendered by the two'; however, it is precisely through this engendering that Hegel affirms a Two which is no longer the pre-philosophical mythical Two, the Two of a symmetrical polarity, but the Two of the non-coincidence of the One with itself." Slavoj Žižek, *Less Than Nothing* (London and New York: Verso, 2012), 840. The most important critical line of thinking here is "that Hegel affirms a Two which is no longer the pre-philosophical mythical Two, the Two of a symmetrical polarity." Meaning, Hegel's dialectic is not the to-and-fro movement between two fixed "things" rather it is the movement of the Whole insofar as the "One" itself is a non-fixed, non-static concept. In short, all identities are composites (of sorts) which make

Introduction 11

identity possible as well as highlight the potential for movement and change, that is, life within identity, subjectivity, personhood, and so on.

4. Slavoj Žižek, *Absolute Recoil: Towards a New Foundation of Dialectical Materialism* (London and New York: Verso, 2014), 1.

5. Fredric Jameson, *Valences of the Dialectic* (London and New York: Verso, 2009), 3.

6. Andrew Douglas, *In the Spirit of Critique: Thinking Politically in the Dialectical Tradition* (New York: State University of New York Press, 2013), 4.

7. This dialectic of archaeology and teleology is theorized by Paul Ricoeur as a hermeneutic of subjectivity, whereas I see it as a matter of ontology. See Paul Ricoeur, *Freud and Philosophy: An Essay on Interpretation* (New Haven and London: Yale University Press, 1970), 342ff.

8. In addition to the many references of logically going "to the end," Žižek self-identifies in the following way: "I always perceived myself as the author of books whose excessively 'witty' texture serves as the envelope of a fundamental coldness, of a 'machinic' deployment of a line of thought which follows its path with utter indifference towards the pathology of so-called human considerations." Slavoj Žižek, *The Žižek Reader*, eds. Elizabeth Wright and Edmond Wright (Oxford and Malden, MA: Blackwell Publishers, 1999), viii, quoted in Rex Butler, *Slavoj Žižek: Live Theory* (New York and London: Continuum, 2005), 13. There is no doubt that Žižek is following the example set by Hegel. As M. W. Jackson makes clear, Hegel self-identifies as "going to the end" which "he himself referred to as 'the severe style' (*der strenge Stil*) that makes no concession to the reader." M. W. Jackson, "Hegel: The Real and the Rational," in *The Hegel Myths and Legends*, ed. Jon Stewart (Evanston: Northwestern University Press, 1996), 19. In explicit terms, Žižek claims that Hegel is the one who, in reference to the incarnation, constructed a "philosophy which thought the implications of the four words ['He was made man'] through to the end." Slavoj Žižek, "The Fear of Four Words: A Modest Plea for the Hegelian Reading of Christianity," in *Monstrosity of Christ: Paradox or Dialectic?* ed. Creston Davis (Cambridge, MA and London: The MIT Press, 2009), 26. See also Žižek, *Less Than Nothing*, 237.

9. By "transition" I mean, in the Hegelian sense, "sublation" insofar as classical interpretations represent a necessary foundation for a critical reinterpretation; therefore, "sublation" is the positive, funding content of classical doctrines that are negated yet preserved to the degree that a critical reinterpretation simultaneously thinks with and beyond a reified theological tradition.

10. Alain Badiou, "Metaphysics and the Critique of Metaphysics," *Pli* 10 (2000): 188. The definition of metaphysics that I propose here is largely informed by Alain Badiou in said article.

11. Frederic Jameson rightfully claims that the "dialectic is not enhanced by its association with the truly vulgar and instrumental idea of method, a temptation we would do well to resist but which is certainly reinforced by the omnipresence of *Verstand* or that reified thinking of which 'method' is so striking an example." Frederic Jameson, *The Hegel Variations: On the Phenomenology of Spirit* (London and New York: Verso, 2010), 4.

12   *Introduction*

12. For Žižek's discussion on overcoming the "prephilosophically naïve" understanding of "thought as a reflection/mirroring of being (of 'independent, objectively existing, reality')," see Slavoj Žižek, *The Parallax View* (Cambridge, MA: The MIT Press, 2006), 6.

13. For example, the pain experienced through political oppression turns into the critical moment necessary for motivating and sustaining political change, and so on. What was first understood as mere negation (pain) is doubled (reflected upon), thus opening up the possibility of real change.

14. Slavoj Žižek, *The Ticklish Subject* (London and New York: Verso, 1999), 231.

15. The creativity of the negative can be seen in its doubling, in its reflexive capacity, which creates a "parallax shift" by way of a change in position and perspective, revealing the constructive capacity of negativity. For example, the pain experienced through political oppression turns into the critical moment used to motivate political change. In other words, what was first understood as simple negation (pain) is doubled (reflected upon), opening a path toward change.

16. G. W. F. Hegel, *Science of Logic*, trans. George Di Giovanni (Cambridge: Cambridge University Press, 2010), 382.

17. Žižek, *Less Than Nothing*, 742.

18. See Hegel, *Science of Logic*, 30ff. Žižek sublates "the standard metaphysical notion of Truth as a substantial In-Itself, independent of the subject's approach to it." Žižek, "The Fear of Four Words," 77.

19. Žižek, "The Fear of Four Words," 77.

20. Regarding my use of "network," I am particularly interested in Mark C. Taylor's use of "complex adaptive networks." As Taylor claims, "deregulated, decentralized, and distributed networks effectively collapse distance and compress time to create a world in which *to be* is to be *connected*. As connectivity spreads, complexity increases and, correlatively, instability and uncertainty grow. These developments, in turn, lead to a longing for simplicity, certainty, and security. Neofoundationalism in all of its guises across the globe represents, among other things, an effort to satisfy this desire." Taylor, *After God*, 3 (emphasis added). Manuel Vasquez argues that network theory is the appropriate model for conceptualizing the present conditions of "complexity, connectivity, and fluidity" as well as "segregation, surveillance, and control." Manuel Vasquez, "Studying Religion in Motion: A Networks Approach," *Method and Theory in the Study of Religion* 20 (2008): 153. For a brief yet insightful history of the term "network," and how it has been employed and defined by various disciplinary fields, see Ernesto Estrada, *The Structure of Complex Networks: Theory and Applications* (Oxford: Oxford University Press, 2011), 3–14. To read Yong's use of network theory in context, see the following examples: Yong, "Tongues of Fire in the Pentecostal Imagination: The Truth of Glossolalia in Light of R. C. Neville's Theory of Religious Symbolism," *Journal of Pentecostal Theology*, Issue 12 (April 1998): 48; Amos Yong, *Discerning the Spirit(s): A Pentecostal-Charismatic Contribution to Christian Theology of Religions* (Sheffield: Sheffield Academic Press, 2000), 252; Yong, *Spirit-Word-Community*, 17; Amos Yong, *Beyond the Impasse: Toward a Pneumatological Theology of Religions* (Grand Rapids: Baker Academic, 2003), 15–16; Amos Yong, *In the Days of Caesar: Pentecostalism and Political*

Theology (Grand Rapids: W. B. Eerdmans, 2010), 5–6; Amos Yong, *The Spirit of Creation: Modern Science and Divine Action in the Pentecostal-Charismatic Imagination* (Grand Rapids: W. B. Eerdmans, 2011), 64.

21. Yong, *Spirit-Word-Community*, 16. See also Yong, *Discerning the Spirit(s)*, 120n27.

22. Yong, *Spirit-Word-Community*, 79.

23. Yong, *Discerning the Spirit(s)*, 120n27.

24. Amos Yong, *The Spirit Poured Out on All Flesh: Pentecostalism and the Possibility of Global Theology* (Grand Rapids, MI: Baker Academic, 2005), 163–4. See also Amos Yong, "Possibility and Actuality: The Doctrine of Creation and Its Implications for Divine Omniscience," *The Wesleyan Philosophical Society Online Journal* 1:1 (2001). http://home.snu.edu/~brint/wpsjnl/Yong01.htm

25. Yong, "Possibility and Actuality."

26. Yong, "Possibility and Actuality."

27. Yong, *Spirit-Word-Community*, 243.

28. Žižek, *For They Know Not What They Do: Enjoyment as a Political Factor* (London; New York: Verso, 1991), 100.

29. Yong, *Spirit-Word-Community*, 86.

30. Yong, *Spirit-Word-Community*, 91.

31. Yong, *Spirit-Word-Community*, 93.

32. Yong, *The Spirit of Creation*, 118–19. Yong identifies C. S. Peirce as a nondualist in *The Spirit Poured Out on All Flesh*, 291.

33. Yong, *The Spirit Poured Out on All Flesh*, 291.

34. Yong, *The Spirit of Creation*, 150–1.

35. Yong, *Discerning the Spirit(s)*, 93.

36. Yong, *The Spirit of Creation*, 71.

37. Yong, *Discerning the Spirit(s)*, 106–7.

38. Yong, *Spirit-Word-Community*, 107.

39. Christopher Stephenson, "Reality, Knowledge, and Life in Community: Metaphysics, Epistemology, and Hermeneutics in the Work of Amos Yong," in *The Theology of Amos Yong and the New Face of Pentecostal Scholarship: Passion for the Spirit*, eds. Wolfgang Vondey and Martin Mittelstadt (Leiden and Boston: Brill, 2013), 81. This critique shows up in two other places in Stephenson's work: his unpublished dissertation and recent monograph. See Christopher Stephenson, *Types of Pentecostal Theology: Method, System, Spirit* (Oxford: Oxford University Press, 2013); and Christopher Stephenson, "Pentecostal Theology According to the Theologians: An Introduction to the Theological Methods of Pentecostal Systematic Theologians," PhD diss., (Marquette University, 2009).

40. This critique is akin to Walter Hollenweger's critique of theological doctrines put forth by Pentecostal institutions: "[M]ost Pentecostal denominations' official statements use out-dated confessional concepts of the turn of the century and pseudo-rationalist thought patterns of the last century which in no way express their dynamic and inspiring spirituality, and which are only magnified by a sometimes frightening Pentecostal triumphalism." Walter Hollenweger, *Pentecostalism: Origins and Developments Worldwide* (Peabody, MA: Hendrickson Publishers, 1997), 202.

14   *Introduction*

41. Stephenson, "Reality, Knowledge, and Life in Community," 81.

42. This retention of infinite subjectivity as other than the world is confusing given Yong's statement elsewhere that "[w]hatever else one may think about the details of Whitehead's cosmology, that we no longer think in the static categories of Hellenistic philosophy scarcely needs to be argued. Given this shift to an ontology of becoming, the fluid nature of thought and language is assumed to reflect the dynamic nature of reality itself." Yong, *Spirit-Word-Community*, 177–8. This critical appraisal seems to separate, in the end, finite from infinite realities.

43. Yong, *The Spirit of Creation*, 163.

44. L. William Oliverio, "An Interpretive Review Essay on Amos Yong's *Spirit-Word-Community: Theological Hermeneutics in Trinitarian Perspective*," *Journal of Pentecostal Theology* 18 (2009): 310.

45. Yong, *Spirit-Word-Community*, 105 (emphasis added).

46. In full, Yong writes: "I am interested in how pneumatology informs and relates to the 'object' of theological knowledge, broadly considered, i.e., God-self-world. (God is certainly not an object, but our experience of God is thematized and in that sense, objectivized, for purposes of reflection, understanding, and communication)." Yong, *Spirit-Word-Community*, 8.

47. Wolfhart Pannenberg asserts, "In contemporary theology one frequently encounters the opinion that rational insight into the ground and content of faith is not only denied us as a matter of fact, but is even injurious to the essence of faith. Faith, one likes to say, must remain a risk. Against this view, I have asserted that the essence of faith must come to harm precisely if in the long run rational conviction about its basis fails to appear. Faith then is easily perverted into blind credulity toward the authority-claim of the preached message; into superstition, owing to its seeming contradiction of better judgment; or even into a tediously wrought work of faith. Therefore, it is precisely for the sake of the purity of faith that the importance of rational knowledge of its basis has to be emphasized." Wolfhart Pannenberg, *Basic Questions in Theology*, vol. 2 (Philadelphia: Fortress Press, 1971), 28.

48. Žižek, *Less Than Nothing*, 66.

49. In the words of LeRon Shults, "a timeless immaterial substance, whose absolute subjectivity is the predetermining first cause of all things." LeRon Shults, *Reforming the Doctrine of God* (Grand Rapids, MI: William B. Eerdmans Publishing Company, 2005), 1.

50. The difference between a classical and postmodern doctrine of God can also be understood in the difference between structuralism and poststructuralism, with the former providing "simplicity, security, and certainty" and the latter providing contingency, complexity, and plasticity. Taylor, *After God*, 3.

51. I am in agreement with Žižek when he claims that "quantum physics . . . undermines our common notion of external reality: beneath the world of simply existing material objects we discover a different reality of virtual particles, of quantum oscillations, of time-space paradoxes, etc., etc.—a wonderful world which, while remaining thoroughly materialistic, is anything but boring. It is, on the contrary, breathtakingly surprising and paradoxical." Slavoj Žižek, "Dialectical Clarity versus the Misty Conceit of Paradox," in *The Monstrosity of Christ: Paradox*

or Dialectic? ed. Creston Davis (Cambridge, MA and London: The MIT Press, 2010), 240.

52. As Mark C. Taylor makes clear, "If the real world is a relational network, it cannot be comprehended through conceptual grids that create divisions and oppositions rather than links and connections. For knowledge to be possible, the structure and development of cognition must be consistent with the structure and development of investigated phenomena. If the mind is wired one way and the world another way, the world as such remains unknowable." Taylor, *After God*, 30.

53. Stephen Houlgate, "Hegel, Desmond, and the Problem of God's Transcendence," *The Owl of Minerva* 36:2 (Spring/Summer 2005): 144.

54. Yong posits the "complex" ontology of "all reality" yet leaves out the "essential complex determinations" of God. Yong, *Beyond the Impasse*, 134.

55. "[T]heology's conviction both that its proper subject matter is God's relationship to all of creation, and, as a corollary, that it (theology) is accountable dialogically to all other branches of human experience and knowledge." Yong, *Spirit-Word-Community*, 100–1.

56. LeRon Shults highlights the three major "conceptual shift[s]" that have occurred in the twentieth century; namely, the revision of "matter, person, and force," changing the future of constructive theology by cutting through the four predominant dichotomies of mind/body, subject/object, God/world, and spirit/matter. In sum, "the basic unit of analysis in contemporary conceptions of personhood is no longer the isolated individual, and the notion of the intellect and will as 'faculties' of a substantial soul has been challenged by neurobiology and other sciences. To be a person is to be in relation." The result of such critical reconceptualization is a critique of discrete categorization, altogether. LeRon Shults, "Spirit and Spirituality: Philosophical Trends in Late Modern Pneumatology," *Pneuma* 30 (2008): 273, 277.

57. Yong, *The Spirit Poured Out on All Flesh*, 136.

Chapter 1

Tracing the Groundwork

AMOS YONG THE THEOLOGIAN

Amos Yong is arguably the leading pentecostal theologian whose influence reaches beyond the confines of pentecostal communities.[1] His intellectual depth, multi- and inter-disciplinary reach, constructive aims, and copious publications validate him as a contemporary theologian worthy of widespread attention.[2] He has put to paper an extensive topological and systematic mapping of pentecostal theology insofar as his pneumatology turns outward rather than inward, thus networking such topics as hermeneutics, phenomenology, epistemology, metaphysics, interreligious dialogue, comparative studies, historical theology, political science, and more.[3] With such a broad scope, he inevitably comes into contact with thinkers from various locations and various times.

As a pentecostal theologian, Yong's work is a viable response to the early call from Walter Hollenweger (the so-called "grandfather of Pentecostal scholarship"[4]) to think through the logical content of the pentecostal experience and refute the reductive accusation that pentecostalism is mere enthusiasm.[5] Yong begins his theology from a "pneumatological starting point" and adheres to the universal accessibility of truth based upon the "foundational" and "public" qualities of pneumatology.[6] Because the Spirit is the point of contact between God and the World, it is through the experience of the Spirit that Yong curates ontological claims. Meaning, through his adherence to the universal accessibility of truth via the Spirit, God is identified as the source, sustainer, and consummator of all life.[7] What emerges with this combination of God-(Spirit)-World is "a *universal* rationality . . . that is consciously *antitotalitarian* precisely because . . . it is pneumatological."[8] The contextual varieties and differences of pneumatological experiences are acknowledged and

18   *Chapter 1*

retained based upon the Spirit being a constant presence and activity in and through the World. Thus, Yong steers clear from monolithic descriptions yet arrives at a universal—albeit contextual—ontology of the Spirit as relational, rational, and dynamic.[9] In other words, Yong "set[s] forth and defend[s] a trinitarian metaphysics that is relational, realistic, and communal."[10]

Trinitarian Theologian

Yong is a trinitarian theologian with a high view of revelation evidenced by the decision to source human thought in the Spirit. In keeping with the economic-immanent delineations of the trinity, he does not completely deny access to the immanent trinity but remains skeptical. Consequently, what humans know about God is given by God, witnessed to by tradition and scripture, and revealed by the illumination of the Spirit. The two theological models that Yong employs to fund this argument are Augustine's Spirit as "the bond of love" and Irenaeus's identification of the Spirit and Son as the "two hands" of God.[11] As Yong explains, "[w]hile [the] mutual love model justifies our starting with the Spirit, the two hands model requires the mutuality and reciprocity of Spirit and Word for theological hermeneutics and method."[12] He privileges these two relational trinitarian models as critiques of social models that lean toward tritheism and separation of persons. By combining Augustine and Irenaeus, he seeks to sustain a hybrid of Western and Eastern emphases on oneness and threeness, respectively, through identity-in-difference, or, as Yong puts it, "relationship-in-autonomy."[13]

Philosophical Theologian

Primarily a theologian, Yong is no less philosophical.[14] He turns to Whitehead and Peirce in the construction of his own epistemology, ontology, and metaphysics. Whitehead's dyad of potentiality and actuality mediated by creativity is endorsed by Yong. However, he critiques the dyad as being a proponent of "conceptual nominalism" insofar as creativity is left without explicit demonstration of how it moves from *potentiality* into *actuality*.[15] To fix this problem, Yong calls upon the field theories of force put forth by Pannenberg, Moltmann, and Welker to demonstrate how disembodied intentionality can impact material reality.[16]

Peirce, though, helps to clarify the intrinsic relation of epistemology and ontology through the triads of Firstness, Secondness, Thirdness[17] and abduction, deduction, and induction.[18] In brief, Peirce crosses the Subject-Object split by way of the "interpretant," that is, the mediator of knower and known,[19] overcoming the "*dualism* [that] leaves things ultimately inexplicable."[20] Yong affirms a Peircean "semiotic metaphysics"[21] wherein language/

Tracing the Groundwork 19

signifier is ontologically connected to reality/signified while asserting an epistemological surplus that preserves mystery. Theologically, this epistemic limitation of human knowing means that all knowledge is grounded in the economic trinity. Furthermore, knowledge is fallibilistic/non-foundational by privileging the experiential and interpretive activities of perception, intuition, and construction in the human connection to, and experience of, the economic activity of God.[22]

Trialectical Methodology

The broad stroke of Yong's methodology is what he calls the "trialectical spiral," which is, namely, "at once biblical, theological, and philosophical; at once metaphysical, epistemological, and hermeneutical."[23] Boiled down, it is simultaneously a "*theological philosophy*—where both the method and material of theology informs the doing of philosophy" and a "*philosophical theology*—where the form and content of metaphysics and epistemology informs the doing of theology."[24] The dialectical flow of his method, then, is a non-hierarchical exchange between theology and philosophy wherein theological claims interrogate and inform philosophical reflection and vice versa[25]—all of such in a simultaneous and spiraling fashion.[26] I am most interested, however, in the critical moment/reversal wherein philosophical claims modify the content of theological experiences, assumptions, concepts, modules, interpretations, and claims. Put differently, I am especially interested in the critical sublation of classical versions of substance theology opposed to complexity.[27]

It would be fitting for Yong to follow Robert Cummings Neville—Yong's dissertation advisor and interlocutor through the early and middle periods of his work—who aims to go beyond "confessional theology that . . . assume[s] some kind of trumping authority for a revelation, tradition, or community," "objective religious studies that avoid[s] the question of truth about first-order theological issues," and anything else that promotes "unchallengeable premise[s]."[28] Indee, Yong argues strongly against the "anti-intellectualist" separation of "faith and thought" with his claim that "mere verbal insistence is nothing without rigorous argumentation."[29] But I become concerned when Yong states that he "*assumes* God is real as the creator and sustainer of this world."[30] Yong's self-described *assumption* that God is the creator and sustainer, if not conceptually coherent with related philosophical claims, cuts against his claim that truth is judged by cohesion and coherence. God as *creator* and *sustainer* must be reconceptualized and redefined to maintain the dialectical system's holistic rationality and coherence; otherwise, dualism persists.

From here, Yong adds to his trinitarian theology and trialectical spiral the "pneumatological imagination," which is the theological disposition

20   *Chapter 1*

that perceives a foundational relation of the human and the Holy Spirit.[31] This concept is important enough for Yong to state that the pneumatological imagination is his "core methodological intuition," which "simply means starting with the Spirit."[32] In other words, the human imagination relies upon the Holy Spirit because "the Holy Spirit is the divine mind that illuminates the rationality of the world to human minds."[33]

The human mind in relation to the divine mind, though, is not entirely passive for Yong. He acknowledges the synthetic and valuational aspects of the human imagination involved in the ability to perceive God. Human intuition and reflection upon objects in the world are thus informed by a "pneumatic"[34] base that involves the human "pragmatic orientation of thinking."[35] Even though persons are only able to understand and respond to the experience of God by way of divine revelation, the human mind must join in the event of understanding. In this sense, God is the creator, sustainer, and consummator by way of the Spirit who is the relational and rational power of life that calls for human participation in the possible knowledge of God.

Therefore, Yong's trinitarian theology, dialectical logic, and divine transcendence exist in relation to his foundational pneumatology, trialectical spiral, and pneumatological imagination. A dialectic is implicitly defined by Yong as a constellation of sources, perspectives, modules, and concepts that are all vital for entering into the fullness of theological understanding and critical theological construction. While Yong employs a dialectical relationship between various disciplines and discourses in his theological project, he chooses to explicitly critique dialectical theologies that privilege one thing over the other(s), which thereby creates obstruction, collapse, and/or a hierarchy of concepts, categories, and perspectives. To combat this problem, Yong claims that the dialectic needs a mediator to sustain the "back-and-forth" movement. Following the claims about the Holy Spirit as the mediator par excellence, Yong believes that the only proper mediator of the dialectic is the Holy Spirit, which maintains a "healthy dialectic" by preventing it from "shutting down."[36] Here, dialectical becomes trialectical insofar as the two poles are enlivened by the central pole/mediator: the Spirit.

Like the Augustinian bond of love with the Spirit as the relation that unites the Father and Son, the Spirit unites all perspectives and concepts in a "synthesis" that preserves identity, distinction, and momentum.[37] It is trinitarian by way of the Irenaean two hands model, which describes the relation of the Son and Spirit as the content (Son) and articulation (Spirit) of creative will (Father).[38] This trinitarian dialectical logic is situated by Yong within a broader triad of Spirit, Word, and Community.[39] Altogether, Yong's schema runs as follows: (1) the dialectic that is sustained by the Spirit (2) gains conceptual and ontological particularity through the revelatory trinitarian relations of Father, Son, and Spirit and (3) is extended into the triad of Spirit,

Word, and Community. Finally, to distinguish and validate his own dialectic, Yong briefly mentions a plethora of modern and contemporary theologians who have fallen from dialectical balance to dialectical distortion.[40] He does this to justify the role of the Holy Spirit in being the force of dialectics. The immanence of the Spirit—within the dialectic—is thus a passageway to the external transcendence of God. Meaning, the being of God is not ontologically impacted by the dialectical relationship between God and World; rather, God plays within the dialectic via Spirit while the essence of God remains external to, that is, ontologically other than, the relationship of God and World.

Divine Transcendence

Divine transcendence thereby retains the classical view that the world has "complete dependence" upon God as the "transcendent source" that creates the world *ex nihilo*. In the end, God will intervene and bring to completion the goal of history: the reconciliation of the World to God. Yong does note, however, the possibility of an essential change in God's being, that is, indetermination to determination, in the act of creation. This query provides the theologian with an avenue for critiquing the classical view of divine transcendence as external to the World, even though Yong does not move into this position.[41] Instead, he cuts off this train of thought based on his belief that such a claim emerges from the vantage point of creation and therefore only seems to be the case.[42] God as transcendent retains its classical distinction in sharp distinction to the finite in that human beings are, in respect to the sui generis of God, essentially contingencies.

Early in his professional career, Yong opened a similar possibility by playing with the idea that it "[may] be the case that the doctrine of the immanent Trinity can be forged alongside the view of God as related rather than prior to creation."[43] The door is opened but quickly shut because the cost is too high. In his opinion, to move into an ontological relation between God and World wherein God is entirely immanent, that is, not external, the outcome is threefold: (1) the onset of an "anemic eschatology," (2) "God's inability to experience us in the depth of our existential subjectivities," and (3) disruption of "a direct encounter with transcendence (divinity) beyond the split between object and subject."[44] In short, Yong maintains a concept of transcendence that preserves the belief that God acts "unilaterally" in relation to the World. As seen in his critique of process theology, Yong is suspicious of the belief that "God does not and cannot unilaterally act in the world" and that "divine action is better understood in terms of co-creation"; this, for Yong, is problematic because of "the ineffectiveness of deity to substantively influence free agents and random events in the world."[45]

22 *Chapter 1*

To avoid the equivocation of divine and human action—and potentially losing the distinction between finite and infinite—he critiques co-creation, opting for the "perlocutionary" dynamic of human participation in divine being insofar as humans are responding to, guided by, and empowered by the Spirit.[46] Transcendence, according to Yong, thereby implies divine existence without any dependence upon the World. Hence, the classical definitions of sovereignty and providence continue to take precedence in defining transcendence.

SLAVOJ ŽIŽEK THE PHILOSOPHER

To extend Yong's theology into comprehensive nondualism, Slavoj Žižek's interpretation of Hegelian dialectics becomes the heuristic critique. This decision is based on theological, philosophical, and constructive reasons. *Theologically*, Yong states that his emphasis upon Spirit, trinity, and dialectics[47] naturally requires him to "come to terms with the influence of Hegel."[48] *Philosophically*, Hegel enacts *the* move out of substance dualism into speculative nondualism. *Constructively*, the Hegelian tradition provides a direct response to the way in which Yong situates the relation of trinity, dialectics, and transcendence. It is Slavoj Žižek who critically interprets and integrates Hegelian ideas on Trinity, dialectic, and transcendence, thereby emerging from the background of thinkers as one of the sharpest and most robust interlocutors for this project.

Theological Grounds

Besides a number of sporadic references to Hegel that are mostly negative, Yong, in his contribution to the Clark Pinnock *Festschrift*, focuses on the potential that Hegel has in relation to his own "pneumatological starting point."[49] He begins by informing the reader that what he presents "should not be mistaken for Hegel scholarship" but interpreted as a "preliminary attempt to re-read Hegel against himself" in the construction of a systematic theology as a first theology of the Holy Spirit.[50] To this end, Yong emphasizes the interrelation of Hegel's (1) critical engagement with Kant in *Faith and Knowledge* and (2) the "Calvary of absolute Spirit" in the final pages of the section on "Absolute Knowing" in the *Phenomenology*, which, according to Yong, identifies *Geist* as the historical activity of the Holy Spirit in the world. Therein, he describes the life and activity of the Spirit as beginning with "self-diremption" and "self-alienation" and through the resurrection, the Spirit makes possible the reconciliation of the World to God. Žižek, however, interprets this Hegelian take on the Passion not as reconciliation between

God and World but as the realization that the two were never separated. For instance, neither the infinite nor the finite predate one another; rather, they emerge simultaneously and dialectically as inherently related amidst a wholly immanent process.

Even though connections with Hegel are already present in Yong (e.g., aspects related to trinity, dialectic, and transcendence), a critical extension of his work is warranted to reach the speculative notion that God is inseparable from the World. To this end, I claim that Yong's philosophical commitments are more conducive to Hegelian insights than he realizes, and that Yong can be critically extended by way of an untapped interface with Žižek and Hegel.[51] Moreover, the aims of Hegel and Yong are similar in that they are both concerned with breaking out of one-sided reification and entering dynamism. Yong's emphases on dialectic, trinitarian theology, relationality, reason, metaphysics, and universality, therefore, all provide the comparative means for a critical and constructive dialogue with the Hegelian tradition in pursuit of nondualism.

Philosophical Grounds

Žižek claims that one should not *return* to Hegel and regurgitate what one finds but *repeat* Hegel in the sense of reinterpreting his theoretical insights that remain relevant to contemporary issues and goals. For example, in the Hegelian adage that "the path towards truth" is "part of the truth" itself.[52] The implication here is that every philosophical system is historical, that is, a "child of its time," thus warranting a critical repetition as context changes in time and place.[53] In general terms, then, Žižek (1) demonstrates the potential of allowing philosophical claims to have full impact upon related theological claims, (2) builds upon the *force of the negative*[54] within the speculative mode of the dialectic, and (3) constructs a speculative, non-substance ontology that plays out in his unique version of dialectical materialism. The shortcoming of Žižek, for my intents and purposes, is a reluctance to enter into a speculative theological reading that follows Hegel's "true infinite" described by J. N. Findlay as an "immanent mysticism."[55] It is the speculative capacity of a theosophic mysticism like that of Eckhart and Boehme which, according to Nicolas Berdyaev, "pertains to God, the world, and [humans]" at the ontological level and not the mysticism of mere experience, feeling, and intuition.[56] To quote Hegel from the *Phenomenology*, "the mystical is not concealment of a secret, or ignorance, but consists in the self knowing itself to be one with the divine Being and that this, therefore, is revealed."[57]

As we're moving in this direction, to properly understand Hegel, one must be able to handle the logical shift that occurs in the transition from Understanding (*Verstand*) to Reason (*Vernunft*).[58] Nicholas Adams succinctly

24   *Chapter 1*

defines it as the move from a "logic of opposition" to a "logic of participation"[59] wherein Thought not only thinks Being but is involved in its Becoming. In effect, what emerges in the speculative moment is an ontology of relationality that no longer holds transcendence as something external or unreachable but inherent. As will eventually become clear(er), speculative reason is *autopoietic*[60] by way of negativity.[61]

To integrate the speculative capacity of the negative is to submit to what J. N. Findlay calls "intellectual crucifixion" or the release from abstract categorical and conceptual distinctions.[62] Indeed, Hegel describes Reason as the "way of despair" due to the pain caused by thought crashing into negativity and contradiction, not only epistemologically but also ontological.[63] Yet, traversing contradictions is necessary in the actualization of truths. As Hegel writes, "only from this error does the truth come forth, and herein lies our reconciliation with error and with finitude."[64]

The Hegelian dialectic of Understanding (*Verstand*) to Reason (*Vernunft*) involves "(a) the Abstract side, or that of understanding, (b) the Dialectical, or that of negative reason; (c) the Speculative, or that of positive reason."[65] Problems arise when thought abstracts from the process and stops at either Understanding or Dialectic, thus missing the Speculative. For example, Understanding is the initial moment of analytic clarity regarding specific categories and finite concepts involved in the dialectic of thought and being. Thought cannot remain in this moment, however, because the mode of observation exists as formal abstraction with categories and concepts that are isolated from one another and independently defined.[66] Therefore, the second moment of the dialectic is the observation of "the one-sidedness and limitation of the predicates of understanding" that exists in Understanding.[67] It is negativity, then, that refutes objective abstraction and conceptual stasis by staying in the dialectical flow of relationality and becoming. Finally, the third moment is the Speculative one wherein the negativity that drives the dialectic is seen as positive in "the Speculative stage, or stage of Positive Reason, apprehend[ing] the unity of terms (propositions) in their opposition—the affirmative, which is involved in their disintegration and in their transition."[68] Speculative reason is the logic of participation amidst Becoming, grounding the dialectic of Being and non-Being. Indeed, speculative reason (*Vernunft*) manifests in and through the actualization of being, refuting the one-sidedness of finitude versus infinitude, thus impacting "the whole terrain of thought."[69] The essence of dialectics, then, is aptly described as the "infinite restlessness" of *Geist*.[70]

Hegel and the Trinity

The Trinity represents a theology of Becoming wherein the relational dynamics of Father, Son, and Spirit demonstrate the processes of (inter) subjectivity.[71] The dialectical relations of trinitarian persons reposition externality within immanence, and divine self-differentiation via Jesus as the Christ is the manifestation of the "monstrous compound" that consists of the finite-infinite dialectic within self-consciousness.[72] In order for self-awareness to exist, acts of differentiation and participation consolidate individuality. The death and resurrection of Jesus are thus a witness to the Hegelian claim that "through the infinite anguish of death comes the infinite love of reconciliation."[73] The resurrection follows by communicating the conceptual integration of death into life, for the Spirit enacts reconciliation amidst separation, thus opening true infinitude wherein the finite and infinite are inherently related and responsible for subjectivity because "the Spirit is identified with the totality of the developmental process."[74] The particularity of the Son embodies negativity in the kenotic incarnation and the confluence of the infinite and the finite within subjectivity. The humanity of Jesus, then, holds ontological impact in the God-World network.[75]

The retention of said religious language does not imply adherence to classical interpretations of such. In the speculative dialectic, thought moves through religious representation (*Vorstellungen*) and into philosophical conceptuality (*Begriffen*) without discarding the former.[76] Meaning, religious language is preserved yet critically redefined for the sake of coherence. To merely accept the theological concepts of *ousia*, *hypostasis*, and *persona* as they have been traditionally defined works against the aid of philosophy in the reconceptualization of Christian nondualism. As Hegel states,

> Theology itself does not know what it wants when it turns against philosophy. Either it carries on unaware of the fact that it needs these forms, that it itself thinks, and that it is a question of proceeding in accord with thought; or it fosters a deception, by reserving for itself the option to think as it chooses.[77]

Dialectical Negativity

To sublate representation, negativity is embraced as the force of dialectical movement and divine identity, which incites a critical change in perspective. Yong nowhere explicitly treats the concept of negativity as productive within a nondualistic ontology, which is one of the reasons why Slavoj Žižek is so important to this argument. Yong does, however, note the reality (not "productivity") of negation in his affirmation of an apophatic dimension within Christian theology.[78] Yong therefore embraces the epistemic experience of negation, not (yet) the ontological reality of negation as productively inherent to both knowers and knowns.

Žižek emphasizes the critical and constructive capacities of the Hegelian "negation of negation," wherein the negative is identified as *difference as*

26   *Chapter 1*

such, thus becoming the "positive ground" necessary for all manifestation(s) of Thought and Being.[79] Meaning, Žižek plays upon the two moments of the speculative dialectic: the *negative dialectic* as destabilizing conceptually static oppositions and the *positive dialectic*, which is a change in perspective (i.e., Žižek's "parallax shift") whereby the negative turns positive in its prevention of conceptual/ontological stasis. Describing this paramount transition that Hegel enacts from simple dialectics to speculative dialectics, Žižek claims that "dialectics *which is not yet speculative* is the vibrant domain of the tremor of reflection and reflexive reversals, the mad dance of negativity . . . ultimately destroy[ing] everything it gives birth to."[80] Speculative logic knows negativity not as something to be overcome and resolved but welcomed.[81] After all, speculative reason is "the rose in the cross of the present" insofar as it holds space for rebirth amidst the terror of death.[82]

The presence of the negative within the speculative dialectic discloses the reality that categories and concepts evolve through "oppositional determination."[83] Žižek's speculative subject reveals the instability, relationality, and composite nature of identity. After that comes an ontology of relationality, plasticity, and complexity vis-à-vis Hegel's True Infinite. Subjectivity develops in the critical transition from subject as isolated being to subject-as-predicate. This move sublates the understanding of subjectivity as that which is objectively static. Hegel claims that "where there is no definite quality, knowledge is impossible. Mere light is mere darkness."[84] In other words, trying to comprehend a subject that is essentially other is impossible. The defining quality of the subject-as-predicate is found in the move from the subject's position to the predicate's position, from the abstract universal subject to the subject-as-predicate.

The subject-as-predicate then returns to—that is, transitions into—the position of the individual subject by way of difference and change. There is no totalizing synthesis here; rather, it is conceptual determination based upon—to use Yong's categories—relationality, rationality, and dynamism. In trinitarian terms, the Father loses its hierarchical, untouchable position (abstract universality) through the incarnation of the Son, who enters historical suffering and death (concrete particularity), and, through resurrection via Spirit, gains individuality (concrete universality). This logical flow necessarily involves the constitutive presence of the World insofar as God is not externally transcendent but immanently composite. Subjectivity, therefore, is not a given substance but a movement that occurs across the dialectic of thought and being toward the self-realization of the finite-infinite. Hence, Žižek points out that "Hegel was the first to elaborate the properly modern notion of *individualization through secondary identification*."[85] The speculative identification of God within the God-World network is actualized through immanence yet retains the mystical quality of distinction amidst connection. In this

Tracing the Groundwork 27

sense, divine personality remains a valid phenomenon only insofar as divine personality is conceptualized in a speculative, nondualistic way. Yong's "relationship-in-autonomy,"[86] then, is preserved yet extended by Žižek, who clarifies that "we conceive identity as an effect of the tissue of differences."[87] It is only through inherent difference(s) that identities exist and communicate. Subjectivity is therefore not a given substance but a rhythmic movement that occurs in the dialectic of Thought and Being—that is, phenomenology, epistemology, and ontology—as human beings are involved in the embodied actualization and realization of God.

Because the presence of negativity exists within the speculative dialectic, relationality emerges through subjectivity as pluralistic and fluctuating. This connects with Yong's "ontology of becoming" and "fluid nature of thought" that reveals "the dynamic nature of reality itself."[88] Yong is right about the correlation of reality and becoming that, if taken to its end, gives way to the speculative moment within trinitarian logic where the *imago dei* binds the rationality of God with the rationality of the World.[89] Not limited to pragmatic "worldmaking," the speculative mode of dialectics and nondualism implies the literal participation of human beings in the becoming existence of God.[90]

Yong knows that there is no pretheoretical experience of God but understandably chooses to avoid it. In a speculative philosophy of religion, God inherits the failures/contradictions that take place through the negative movement of dialectical logic in and through concrete particularity. It comes down to whether the theologian agrees with the watershed critiques that Immanuel Kant proposed against natural theology and revealed theology. The theologian will either turn to practical reason as the location of God (as did Kant) and continue to espouse the unknowability of God or follow Hegel into a speculative philosophy of religion wherein the concept of God is changed from an external thing-in-itself to the rich relationship of the finite and the infinite. If so, the content of traditional theology will undergo conceptual change for systematic theology to be both public and scientific. For theology to be public—to be multi- and inter-disciplinary—it must be freed from a vicious hermeneutic circle wherein theological sources such as scripture, tradition, experience, and reason remain in their precritical settings. For theology to be scientific—that is, to be rational—it must prevail over the fear of change when "the basic framework itself undergoes a transformation."[91]

Put succinctly, Žižek's speculative dialectic provides the means for a critical revision of Yong's pneumatological starting point and corollary retention of God as external to the World, thereby discovering new contours of trinitarian theology in the God-World network. The speculative dialectic enhances Yong's inter- and multi-disciplinary theology, trinitarian metaphysic, and ontologies of relationality, rationality, and dynamism, thus bridging the gap

28 *Chapter 1*

between theological reflection (epistemology) and truth (ontology) without reduction into panentheism, pantheism, or atheism. My solution is not the simple turn to process theology; rather, it is a deepening of—a tapping into, rather—the speculative mode of dialectics that are already at play.

NOTES

1. I follow Yong's use of lowercase "p" in pentecostal to signify not just the classical, charismatic, and neo-pentecostal movements, which emphasize (1) the Luke-Acts composition, (2) pneumatological theology, and (3) pneumatological praxis, but also the openness of a Spirit disposition. See Yong, *Spirit-Word-Community*, 18–29.

2. Steven Studebaker claims that Yong's unique contribution to contemporary theology is a "pneumatological trinitarian theology." Steven Studebaker, "Toward a Pneumatological Trinitarian Theology: Amos Yong, the Spirit, and the Trinity," in *The Theology of Amos Yong and the New Face of Pentecostal Scholarship: Passion for the Spirit*, eds. Wolfgang Vondey and Martin Mittelstadt (Leiden and Boston: Brill, 2013), 83.

3. In the words of L. William Oliverio, "More than any major Pentecostal theologian before him, Yong has dwelled in the pluralities and the differences, playing around like a fox with various disciplines of inquiry, perspectives, contexts, and traditions. Characteristic of his work is the readiness to dialogue with perspectives from outside his own traditions. Yong moves from theology of religions to hermeneutics, from metaphysics to ontology to pneumatological theology in global contexts, from theology of disability to interreligious practices, from political theology to theology and science." L. William Oliverio, "The One and the Many: Amos Yong and the Pluralism and Dissolution of Later Modernity," in *The Theology of Amos Yong and the New Face of Pentecostal Scholarship: Passion for the Spirit*, eds. Martin Mittelstadt and Wolfgang Vondey (London and Boston: Brill, 2013), 45–6.

4. L. William Oliverio, *Theological Hermeneutics in the Classical Pentecostal Tradition: A Typological Account* (Leiden and Boston: Brill, 2012), 14.

5. In his first monograph, Yong writes: "Hollenweger does not take issue with Cox's theory of religion. Instead, among other suggestions, he urges Cox to give Pentecostals more credit than he does for their developing theological sophistication. Implicitly, Hollenweger's review . . . constitutes a challenge to Pentecostals to grapple more seriously from a theological perspective." Yong, *Discerning the Spirit(s)*, 18n2.

6. Amos Yong, "A Theology of the Third Article? Hegel and the Contemporary Enterprise in First Philosophy and First Theology," in *Semper Reformandum: Studies in Honour of Clark H. Pinnock,* eds. Stanley E. Porter and Anthony R. Cross (Carlisle: Paternoster Press, 2003), 224–5. See also: Amos Yong, "On Divine Presence and Divine Agency: Toward a Foundational Pneumatology," *Asian Journal of Pentecostal Studies* 3, no. 2 (July 2000): 167–88.

7. Yong, "On Divine Presence and Divine Agency," 167–88.

8. Yong, *Spirit-Word-Community*, 84 (emphasis added).

Tracing the Groundwork
29

9. Yong, *Discerning the Spirit(s)*, 112; *Spirit-Word-Community*, 28–48.

10. Yong, *Spirit-Word-Community*, 25.

11. In the words of Yong, "It should now be clearer that while on the theological level the Spirit is the divine person who mediates Father and Son—in Augustine's terms, the Spirit is the love that binds together Lover and the Beloved (*De Trinitate* 15.17.29)—in Peirce's semiotic framework, the Spirit interprets the creator to creation (and vice versa). In other words, our experience of the world and the emerging interpretations thereof point to the creator. In this scheme of things, the Spirit is the supreme relation between us as knowers and the self-revealing God. As supreme relation, the Spirit is also non-objectifiable and therefore only accessible symbolically." Yong, *Discerning the Spirit(s)*, 114; Yong, *Spirit-Word-Community*, 71–2.

12. Yong, *Spirit-Word-Community*, 220.

13. Yong, *Discerning the Spirit(s)*, 70. Regarding trinitarian conceptualization, Yong critiques the Western *filioque* and its subordination of Spirit to Son: "if indeed the filioque is reasserted, pneumatology may remain subordinated to Christology, thereby minimally securing the fulfillment theory—the notion that other faiths, including Judaism, are valid only as anticipations of the Christian revelation and therefore are fulfilled by Christ—and perhaps reinforcing the Catholic doctrine of *extra ecclesiam nulla salus*." Yong, *Discerning the Spirit(s)*, 186.

14. Yong self-describes as a systematic theologian and expounds on what this means in Amos Yong, "Whither Systematic Theology? A Systematician Chimes in on a Scandalous Conversation," *Pneuma: The Journal of the Society for Pentecostal Studies* 20:1 (Spring 1998): 85–93.

15. Yong, *Spirit-Word-Community*, 89–90.

16. Yong mentions Pannenberg, Moltmann, and Welker in this regard. See Yong, *Discerning the Spirit(s)*, 117; Yong, *Beyond the Impasse*, 136n9; Yong, *Spirit-Word-Community*, 90.

17. Playing with C. S. Peirce's category of Thirdness, the Spirit is the dynamic universality of the dialectic of potentiality (Firstness/Father) and actuality (Secondness/Son). Yong, *Spirit-Word-Community*, 95; Yong, *Beyond the Impasse,* 133.

18. Amos Yong, "The Demise of Foundationalism and the Retention of Truth: What Evangelicals Can Learn from C. S. Peirce," *Christian Scholar's Review* 29:3 (Spring 2000): 573–8.

19. Yong, *Spirit-Word-Community*, 22.

20. Yong, "The Demise of Foundationalism and the Retention of Truth," 570n20 (emphasis added).

21. Yong, *The Spirit Poured Out on All Flesh*, 288.

22. Yong writes on the contribution of C. S. Peirce to theology: "In sum, getting at the truth involves the logic of reasoning, the continuous fallible activity of a community of inquirers, beginning physiologically with vague perceptual mental signs, proceeding cognitively via abduction, deduction, and induction in rendering them more completely determinate, and while never getting thought to correspond directly to its object, always increasingly approximating this concordance through the potentially indefinite process of inquiry, which terminates when a certain degree of action is made possible and doubt is minimized. The proof of pragmatism, as

Peirce understood it, lies in its following the logic of reasoning. This logic enables the community of inquirers to decipher signs of themselves and the world, interpret experience, clarify meanings, understand intellectual concepts, be habituated to reality, and apprehend truth." Yong, "The Demise of Foundationalism and the Retention of Truth," 578.

23. Yong, *Spirit-Word-Community*, 24.

24. Yong, *Spirit-Word-Community*, 20 (emphasis added).

25. "The conjunction between trinitarian theology, metaphysics and epistemology derives from my conviction that the goal of a theological hermeneutics cannot be accomplished by subordinating metaphysical and epistemological considerations in a simplistic sense to theological ones." Yong, *Spirit-Word-Community*, 19.

26. "The pneumatological starting point means not that the order of the argument is sacrosanct, but that the central categories of the argument are intrinsic, coinhering and mutually defining." Yong, *Spirit-Word-Community*, 24.

27. Yong is consistently open to critiques of theological presuppositions and assumptions. "Our criteriologies should be recognized for what they are: human constructions—our best efforts to discern the Spirit of God from the demonic in our world of flux—even as we attempt to faithfully rely upon, listen to, and follow the Spirit. To that extent, a humble and faithful reliance on God to shatter our preconceptions and assumptions is in order." Amos Yong, *Beyond the Impasse*, 159. I want to emphasize, though, that if Yong identifies philosophy as influenced by God, then philosophy can also "shatter" theological "preconceptions and assumptions." Yong demonstrates this philosophical capacity with his consistent critique of the "assumed dualism between matter and spirit" and blunt claim that "there is no room for metaphysical dualism in any theology of the Holy Spirit informed by the Pentecostal-charismatic experience." Yong, *Discerning the Spirit(s)*, 172, 175.

28. Robert Cummings Neville, *Ultimates: Philosophical Theology*, vol. 1 (New York: State University of New York Press, 2013), xv, xvii.

29. Yong, "Whither Systematic Theology?" 87–8, 92.

30. Yong, *Spirit-Word-Community*, 3 (emphasis added).

31. See Yong, "On Divine Presence and Divine Agency," 167–88.

32. Amos Yong, *The Cosmic Breath: Spirit and Nature in the Christianity-Buddhism-Science Trialogue* (Leiden; Boston: Brill, 2012), xiii.

33. Yong, *Spirit-Word-Community*, 123.

34. See Yong, *Discerning the Spirit(s)*, 103; *Spirit-Word-Community*, 7, 134, 139, 229.

35. Yong, *Spirit-Word-Community*, 132.

36. Yong, *Spirit-Word-Community*, 14.

37. As Yong writes, "Throughout the argument so far, spirit has been understood as that relational category which enables synthesis of two (or more) terms or poles (thus being trialectical) while preserving the integrity of the two terms synthesized. Thus the advantage of a pneumatological approach to metaphysics and ontology is that it a) requires and demands the universal emphasis on the particularity, concreteness and individuality of things; b) highlights the dialectical relationship which characterizes the social and processive nature of things and serves as the dynamic that

drives the back-and-forth movement of the creative process; and c) moves toward a non-duality whereby the particularities of both sides are retained and acknowledged." Yong, *Spirit-Word-Community*, 117.

38. The problem, according to Žižek, is that the understanding of the Son and Spirit as extensions of the Father retains classical theism's idea that the Father oversees the Son and Spirit and is therefore the big Other, that is, the external, isolated divine object that exists on its own and absolutely resists the World's participation in the being of God.

39. The order of Spirit, Word, and Community is non-hierarchical and therefore also spirating. See Yong, *Spirit-Word-Community*, 15–18.

40. Regarding James A. Sanders, Charles Dickinson, Francis Watson, R. W. L. Moberly, Anthony Thiselton, Francis Schussler Fiorenza, Ormand Rush, James Callahan, Kevin Vanhoozer, Stanley Grenz, and John Franke, Yong claims that "what is missing from each of these otherwise valuable contributions is a robust pneumatology to sustain the triadic movement." Yong, *Spirit-Word-Community*, 10. Regarding Gordon Kaufman, Paul Tillich, Karl Rahner, Wolfhart Pannenberg, David Tracy, LeRon Shults, and Donald Bloesch, Yong claims that they are all victims of collapsing the dialectic into a hierarchy insofar as "one side of the dialectic imposes its authority over the other side resulting in the subordination of the latter and the breakdown of the dialectic." Yong, *Spirit-Word-Community*, 12.

41. "The problem of the one and the many hence leads to the speculative metaphysical hypothesis of God as the indeterminate, or transcendent, creator of all things *ex nihilo*. Classical Christian theology has therefore been correct in emphasizing the divine transcendence and the complete dependence of the world on such a transcendent source. This is the theological truth at the heart of the Christian doctrine of creation *ex nihilo*." Yong, *Discerning the Spirit(s)*, 106–7.

42. "Creation *ex nihilo*, however, means that divine creating is free and, from our vantage point, arbitrary. God, in this view, is determinate only in relation to his creating the world. To be more specific, God gives Godself the feature of creator only in the act of creating. To attempt to speak of divinity apart from creation is to attempt to predicate something of what is essentially indeterminate. Recall that determinateness is what it is only because of the creative act. Because of this, we cannot get behind the creative act to discern the reasons for creation." Yong, *Discerning the Spirit(s)*, 106–07.

43. Amos Yong, "Oneness and the Trinity: The Theological and Ecumenical Implications of 'Creation Ex Nihilo' for an Intra-Pentecostal Dispute," *PNEUMA* 19:1 (Spring 1997): 107.

44. Yong, *Spirit-Word-Community*, 93n38.

45. Yong, *Discerning the Spirit(s)*, 93.

46. Yong, *The Spirit of Creation*, 101.

47. What he calls his "pneumatological-trinitarian hermeneutic," "pneumatological-trinitarian epistemology," and "pneumatological-trinitarian metaphysic." Yong, *Spirit-Word-Community*, 19.

48. Yong writes, "Any attempt at a foundational pneumatology will inevitably be likened to Hegel's quest as found in his *Phenomenology of Spirit* and other works

32   *Chapter 1*

(mine certainly was, as remarked upon by one of my dissertation readers)." Yong, "On Divine Presence and Divine Agency," 188n35. And later, "When I first began doing work in pneumatological theology, I had already intuited then that at some point, I would need to come to terms with the influence of Hegel—for better or worse—for this project. . . . This essay is the first fruits of an anticipated book-length effort to confront the specter of Hegel in contemporary first philosophy and first theology." Yong, "A Theology of the Third Article?" 210n4.

49. Yong, "A Theology of the Third Article?" 224–5.

50. Yong, "A Theology of the Third Article?" 210. This interpretation of Hegel is akin to what John Milbank calls "theopneumatic." John Milbank, "The Second Difference: For a Trinitarianism without Reserve," *Modern Theology* 2:3 (1986): 213.

51. The Hegelian schools of thought and their respective interpreters cannot be reduced and flattened into singularity.

52. Žižek, *Less Than Nothing*, 503–4.

53. Hegel writes, "To comprehend *what is* is the task of philosophy, for *what is*, is reason. As far as the individual is concerned, each individual is in any case a *child of his time*; thus philosophy, too, is *its own time comprehended in thoughts*. It is just as foolish to imagine that any philosophy can transcend its contemporary world as that an individual can overleap his own time or leap over Rhodes. If his theory does indeed transcend his own time, if it builds itself a world *as it ought to be*, then it certainly has an existence, but only within his opinions—a pliant medium in which the imagination can construct anything it pleases." G. W. F. Hegel, *Elements of the Philosophy of Right*, trans. H. B. Nisbet (Cambridge: Cambridge University Press, 2003), 21–2.

54. As Žižek likes to say, is the force that generates *something out of nothing*, that is, the force of that which is less than nothing.

55. J. N. Findlay, *Hegel: A Re-Examination* (New York: Humanities Press, 1964), 68. In Hegel's own words, "Speculative truth . . . means very much the same as what, in special connection with religious experience and doctrines, used to be called Mysticism. . . [T]he mystical, as synonymous with the speculative, is the concrete unity of those propositions which understanding only accepts in their separation and opposition." G. W. F. Hegel, *Encyclopaedia Logic*, trans. William Wallace (Oxford: Oxford University Press, 1975), §81.

56. Nicolas Berdyaev, "Introduction," in Jacob Boehme, *Six Theosophic Points and Other Writings* (Ann Arbor, MI: University of Michigan Press, 1958), v–xxxvii, vii.

57. G. W. F. Hegel, *Phenomenology of Spirit*, trans. A. V. Miller (Oxford: Oxford University Press, 1977), §722.

58. For example, Mark C. Taylor claims that "Hegel's entire systematic enterprise turns on a distinction between understanding (*Verstand*) and reason (*Vernunft*). Understanding, which is based upon the principle of noncontradiction, is the analytic activity by which one makes distinction, establishes antitheses and discerns paradoxes. . . . Reason, by contrast, apprehends the dialectical interplay of differences; when rationally comprehended, differences are not exclusive but are codependent and, therefore, coevolve." Mark C. Taylor, "Infinite Restlessness," in *Hegel and the*

Infinite: Religion, Politics, and Dialectic, eds. Slavoj Žižek, Clayton Crockett, and Creston Davis (New York: Columbia University Press, 2011), 92–3.

59. Nicholas Adams, *Eclipse of Grace: Divine and Human Action in Hegel* (Hoboken, NJ: Wiley-Blackwell, 2013), 225.

60. Autopoiesis as "no preexisting necessity that directs the dialectical process, since this necessity is precisely what arises through this process, i.e., what this process is about." Žižek, "Dialectical Clarity versus the Misty Conceit of Paradox," 246. And, regarding "autopoietic self-organization," Žižek writes: "The subject is thus, at its most radical, not the agent of the process: the agent is the System (of knowledge) itself, which 'automatically' deploys itself without any need for external pushes or impetuses." Slavoj Žižek, *The Sublime Object of Ideology* (London and New York: Verso, 1989/2008), xv.

61. Jean-Luc Nancy, an expert on the power of the negative in Hegel's dialectical logic, writes: "Ordeal, misery, restlessness, and task of thought: Hegel is the witness of the world's entry into a history in which it is no longer just a matter of changing form, of replacing one vision and one order by some other vision and some other order, but in which the one and only point—of view and of order—is that of transformation itself. It is thus not a point; it is the passage, the negativity in which the cutting edge of sense gets experienced as never before." Jean-Luc Nancy, *Hegel: The Restlessness of the Negative* (Minneapolis: University of Minnesota Press, 2002), 6–7.

62. J. N. Findlay, *Hegel: A Re-Examination* (New York: Humanities Press, 1964), 25.

63. Hegel, *Phenomenology of Spirit*, §78.

64. G. W. F. Hegel, *The Encyclopaedia Logic (with the Zusätze): Part I of the Encyclopaedia of Philosophical Sciences*, trans. T. F. Geraets, W. A. Suchting, and H. S. Harris (Indianapolis and Cambridge: Hackett Publishing Company, Inc., 1991), §212.

65. Hegel, *The Encyclopedia Logic*, §79.

66. Hegel writes, "Consequently, this abstract Understanding has turned against all determinateness, has emptied Truth of all content whatever so that nothing remains for it except, on the one hand, the pure negative, the *[dead head]* of a merely abstract *Being.* . . . From such a God there is nothing to be had for He has already been emptied of all content. He is the Unknowable, for knowledge has to do with a determinate content, with movement; but the void lacks a content, is indeterminate and possesses no immanent life and action." G. W. F. Hegel, "Reason and Religious Truth," in *Die Religion im inneren Verhaltnisse zur Wissenschaft* (1822), H. Fr. W. Hinrichs. Quoted in *Beyond Epistemology*, ed. Frederick Weiss, trans. A. V. Miller (Hague: Martinus Nijhoff, 1974), 231–2.

67. Hegel, *The Encyclopaedia Logic*, §81.

68. Hegel, *The Encyclopaedia Logic*, §82.

69. Žižek, *The Ticklish Subject* (London and New York: Verso, 1999), 231.

70. Jean-Luc Nancy, *Hegel: The Restlessness of the Negative* (Minneapolis: University of Minnesota Press), 8. For more on this important distinction, see Mark C. Taylor, "Infinite Restlessness," in *Hegel and the Infinite: Religion, Politics, and Dialectic*, eds. Slavoj Žižek, Clayton Crockett, and Creston Davis (New York: Columbia University

Press, 2011), 92–3, and Žižek, *For They Know Not What They Do*, 138n19. On the dialectical transition from Understanding to Reason, see Slavoj Žižek, *The Ticklish Subject* (London; New York: Verso, 1999), 85–6; Žižek, *Sublime Object of Ideology,* ix; Žižek, *Less than Nothing*, 188, 280, 380; and Slavoj Žižek, *The Most Sublime Hysteric: Hegel with Lacan,* trans. Thomas Scott-Railton (Cambridge: Polity, 2014), 10–11.

71. See section three, "The Consummate Religion," in *G. W. F. Hegel, Lectures on the Philosophy of Religion: One Volume Edition. The Lectures of 1827,* ed. Peter C. Hodgson, trans. R. F. Brown, P. C. Hodgson, and J. M. Stewart (Berkeley, CA: University of California Press, 1988).

72. Hegel, *Lectures on the Philosophy of Religion,* 457–8. See also Peter Hodgson, *Hegel & Christianity: A Reading of the Lectures on the Philosophy of Religion* (Oxford: Oxford University Press, 2005), 90. In the words of Hegel, "only the absolute idea determines itself and is certain of itself as absolutely free within itself because of this self-determination." Hegel, *Lectures on the Philosophy of Religion,* 434.

73. Hodgson, *Hegel & Christianity,* 276.

74. Douglas Finn, *Life in the Spirit: Trinitarian Grammar and Pneumatic Community in Hegel and Augustine* (Notre Dame: University of Notre Dame Press, 2016), 25.

75. Douglas Finn helps to unpack this a bit when he writes that "Hegel conceives of God as fully active not in a sense exclusive of all potentiality, but as a necessary developmental process of self-manifestation and actualization, of movement from abstraction and implicitness to the determinate reality and explicit knowledge of who God is as personality. While God as Father is already implicitly active in that revelatory dynamic—an implicit activity whereby Hegel can establish the identity of beginning and end in the process of divine becoming—that immanent movement remains abstract, a universal sans content that has not yet entered into relationship with a genuine other. Hence God 'creates' the world." Douglas Finn, *Life in the Spirit: Trinitarian Grammar and Pneumatic Community in Hegel and Augustine* (Notre Dame: University of Notre Dame Press, 2016), 27.

76. Nancy, *Hegel,* 34–35.

77. Hegel, *Lectures on the Philosophy of Religion,* 401.

78. See Yong, *Discerning the Spirit(s),* 119n26; Yong, *Spirit-Word-Community,* 211–13.

79. "[I]n contrast to a mere difference between objects, *the pure difference is itself an object*"; one that is unable to be captured by the symbolic order and therefore constantly disrupts consistency; "a 'pure' difference which cannot be grounded in positive substantial properties." Žižek, *The Parallax View,* 18. See also Žižek, *Less Than Nothing,* 502.

80. Slavoj Žižek, *Absolute Recoil: Towards a New Foundation of Dialectical Materialism* (London and New York: Verso, 2014), 16 (emphasis added).

81. Žižek, *Less Than Nothing,* 403.

82. Hegel, *Elements of the Philosophy of Right,* 22.

83. Žižek, *For They Know Not What They Do,* xxvi. See also Slavoj Žižek, *Tarrying with the Negative: Kant, Hegel, and the Critique of Ideology* (Durham: Duke University Press, 1993), 132, 139; *Less Than Nothing,* 456, 501.

Tracing the Groundwork   35

84. Hegel, *The Encyclopedia Logic*, §36.

85. Žižek, *The Ticklish Subject*, 90.

86. Yong, *Discerning the Spirit(s)*, 70.

87. Žižek, *Tarrying with the Negative*, 124.

88. Yong, *Spirit-Word-Community*, 178.

89. On the phrase followed through, Žižek describes the "deployment of a line of thought" as "follow[ing] its path with utter indifference." Slavoj Žižek, *The Žižek Reader*, eds. Elizabeth Wright and Edmond Wright (Oxford and Malden, MA: Blackwell Publishers, 1999), viii, quoted in Rex Butler, *Slavoj Žižek: Live Theory* (New York and London: Continuum, 2005), 13. See also Žižek, "The Fear of Four Words," 26; Žižek, *Less Than Nothing*, 237; and M. W. Jackson, "Hegel: The Real and the Rational," in *The Hegel Myths and Legends*, ed. Jon Stewart (Evanston: Northwestern University Press, 1996), 19.

90. Yong, *Spirit-Word-Community*, 134, 146–7.

91. Žižek, *The Sublime Object of Ideology*, vii. See also Žižek, *Less Than Nothing*, 715.

Chapter 2

Amos Yong on Trinity, Dialectics, and Transcendence

THEORIZING AMOS YONG

In my reading of Yong, his theology consists of three core concepts—trinity, dialectic, and transcendence—and three core modules—foundational pneumatology, trialectical spiral, and pneumatological imagination. Each has its own function and set of components, but to observe the structure of Yong's theology, they must be dealt with as a package for paradigmatic change to occur; otherwise, one is left dealing with disconnected pieces bereft of momentum. For example, in his first publication, *Discerning the Spirit(s)*, Yong (1) deals with the primary experience of the Spirit within the *trinitarian* paradigm, (2) touches the *dialectical* quality of relationality, (3) unpacks the categories of divine *transcendence* in light of creation and human freedom, (4) traces a *foundational pneumatology* that undergirds a pneumatological theology of religions, (5) describes the creative participation of the world in the *pneumatological imagination*, and (6) traces all of these within the *trialectical spiral*. This distinct approach continues to be clarified and enhanced throughout his work.

Yong's systematic theology is packed with various moving parts, thus requiring commitment and perseverance from the reader. Part of the complexity one finds in Yong's work has to do with his awareness of the general interrelationality of concepts and modules, which manifests in his work as multi- and inter-disciplinary emphases.[1] The philosophical implication of Yong's multi-faceted theology is, in general, nondualism.[2] It makes sense to expect no hard break between subject and object and/or God and World. It would also make sense to expect that, for Yong, method and content are interrelated, that is, that method does not structure the way *toward* content that exists somewhere else, but that method *reflects* upon the content that it is

38   *Chapter 2*

already participating in. Yong consistently endorses nondualism, but he does not go far enough. Such would seek to get comfortable inside the liminal space that exists in between identities that are formed through relational difference, including the identities of God and World.

Yong privileges dualism, though, when he confesses that a "radical alterity"[3] exists between knowers and knowns.[4] To be nondualistic is to assert that Subject(s) and Object(s) are not other than one another but that they are joined by way of (speculative) negativity. The problem is that radical alterity funds a "radical transcendence," which Yong describes as "a reminder that the Spirit's activity is unpredictable, and that the Spirit's field of force cannot be identified *in toto* with the public force of creation."[5] So, why assert a radical alterity if known to promote dualism? Because, according to Yong, what needs to be preserved is an eschatological openness that is guided by the Holy Spirit "beyond our respective horizons."[6] Said differently, the economic roles of the trinity *do* reveal truths about the internal subjectivity of God but only in a partially detached way.[7] Yong wants to isolate the essence of God and put it into its own space of being in order to keep God autonomous. Unfortunately, it does so at the expense of nondualism.

Put differently, the economic trinity reveals truths about the immanent trinity with remainder.[8] In short, persons have epistemological access to the being of God by way of God's activity in history, yet this truth reaches its limit in that one cannot comprehend the essence of God that exists separate from historical activity. For Yong, there is always an excess of God beyond both experience and knowledge. Hence, Yong believes that his conceptualization of transcendence is nondualistic insofar as human beings *do* have some access to God. However, this human knowledge of God is made possible by the joint revelation of scripture and the illumination of the Spirit and not because of any ontological participation of human beings in the being of God.[9] Human beings are therefore not in direct relation to God because it is God who is responsible for that relationship. Meaning, human beings only know what God allows them to know, and that which is known about God is laden with errors. Along this path, Yong is comfortable with constructing a trinitarian-based metaphysic that extends into a "trialectic"[10] of God, Self, and the World albeit always privileging God as the ultimate source.[11]

Nevertheless, Yong endorses "the interrelationship between the various dimensions of reality"[12] and endorses the nondualisms of transcendence and immanence,[13] God and World,[14] mind and body,[15] spirit and matter,[16] "material and non-material,"[17] subject and object,[18] ontology,[19] reason and experience,[20] reason and affection,[21] natural and supernatural,[22] sacred and secular,[23] and church and world.[24] Yong even states that "there is no room for metaphysical dualism in any theology of the Holy Spirit informed by the Pentecostal-charismatic experience."[25] Therefore, I want to be clear that I am not forcing

Yong in any direction that he is not already moving in. It is my claim that he has not yet moved far enough down the logical path that he is constructing; thus, substance dualism continues to be a problem in his theology.

Regarding his trinitarian theology, while it is true that Amos Yong, as a pentecostal theologian, is highly attuned to the role of the Holy Spirit in Christian theology and anthropology, it is far more appropriate to say that Yong is a *trinitarian* theologian insofar as his theological gaze emerges from the initial experience of the Spirit realized as being set within a broader trinitarian theology, that is, a "trinitarian metaphysics of creation."[26] In his first monograph, *Discerning the Spirit(s)*, Yong is quick to set straight any potential confusion that would interpret his pentecostal roots and emphasis upon the Spirit as subordination of the Father and the Son to the Spirit. Simply put, "Christology and pneumatology must be understood within a broader trinitarian framework."[27] Yong is therefore not concerned with developing a singular doctrine of the Holy Spirit without other theological loci; rather, his work is highly attuned to the experience of the Spirit that always-already implies the interrelations and implications of Father and Son. Even if Yong claims that the human experience of God begins with the experience of the Spirit, one can retroactively interpret this experience of the Spirit as including the broader participation of trinitarian persons within the hermeneutical context of Self and World. Yong's foundational pneumatology thus recognizes the ontological relations of the Trinity and spirit(s) of the world wherein the Holy Spirit is dialectically related to everything insofar as the Spirit is continuously unfolding in and through the World.

This does not mean that the Holy Spirit is conceived as existing apart from the Father and the Son. Yong walks the fine line of sameness and difference between Father, Son, and Spirit. His trinitarian thought works to avoid the two theological ditches of conflation (i.e., monarchial modalism) and separation (i.e., tritheism) by treating each divine being as unique amidst ontological interrelationality. This can be seen by way of two types of comments: the first as preserving trinitarian difference[28] and the second as preserving trinitarian sameness.[29] Yong is, therefore, critical of social trinitarian models because of the potential separation of the Father, Son, and Spirit that results in tritheism. In response, Yong maintains a relational trinity that turns upon the nuances of a dialectical "relationship-in-autonomy"[30] and "relationship-in-distinction."[31] This "trinitarian perichoretic relationality"[32] unfolds as dialectical insofar as the Father, Son, and Spirit achieve identity through relational differentiation, that is, through "unity-in-diversity."[33] Ultimately, it is the Spirit that is the relational bond that unites the Father and the Son as well as God and the World.

The ontological quality of the Holy Spirit as relational, rational, and dynamic, that is, as the lynchpin that binds Father and Son while sustaining

40   *Chapter 2*

and giving shape to the World, is the entryway into what Yong means when he says that he "set[s] forth and defend[s] a trinitarian metaphysics that is relational, realistic, and communal."[34] By metaphysical, Yong, in short, means the way(s) in which the trinity is "related to the world."[35] This metaphysical trinitarian theology of the God-World relationship is worked out in the theological modules of a foundational pneumatology that exists in the background of the human pneumatological imagination which guides the human mind amidst the trialectical spiral of knowledge.

TRINITY

One of the trinitarian models that Yong builds his theological form and content around is Irenaeus's "two hands of God" metaphor.[36] First, the two hands model emphasizes the human/theological entry point as being connected to the economic Trinity, thus leaving the immanent somewhat detached to preserve the transcendence of God. Second, it emphasizes the presence and activity of the Spirit in the world insofar as the Spirit is directly named as one hand of the Father. Third, and related to this, it emphasizes the non-subordination of the Spirit to the Son with its emphasis upon the "dialectic of Word and Spirit," thus avoiding conflation of one into the other yet preserving their ontological coinherence.[37] Fourth, what Yong adds to this two hands model that is not made explicit by Irenaeus but is there for the taking is the inclusion of the Self and the World insofar as the presence and activity of the Spirit and the Son only happen amidst the cosmic community.[38] This grand Irenaean vision is the core of Yong's big book on method, *Spirit-Word-Community*.

With the Spirit as his entryway, one of the justifications of Yong's preference for "starting with the Spirit" is a critical reaction against the traditional trend of "knowing and rationality" being "connected to the Logos" and not also to the Spirit; at least, not dialectically.[39] Yong's "pneumatological imagination"—one of Yong's key theological modules—demonstrates a critical reappropriation of knowledge and rationality as also founded and sustained by the Spirit. Thus, the "foundational" and/or metaphysical qualities/concepts of the Spirit in Yong's "foundational pneumatology" are relationality, rationality, and dynamism. Point blank, the Spirit *is* relational, rational, and dynamic.[40] Not at the expense of the Word, though, insofar as the Holy Spirit exists interdependently vis-à-vis Son and Father. In one case, the Son is translated as the concreteness or "thisness" and the Spirit as the "whatness" or "relatedness" within a dialectical ontology of the conjoined Augustinian and Irenaean trinitarian models.[41] Elsewhere, Yong simply defines the dialectical interplay of "Spirit and Word" as the two modes of identity: "spirituality and materiality."[42] Overall, Yong is interested in demonstrating the trinitarian structure of reality wherein the Father, Son, and Spirit have unique aspects that are inextricable from one another.[43]

SPIRIT

Even still, Yong always begins with the Spirit given his pentecostal identity and the conviction that the primary contact that human beings have with God is mediated through the Spirit. In Yong's own words, because of the "prevenient presence and activity of God through the Holy Spirit."[44] As such, he begins to answer the question "Who is the Holy Spirit?" by identifying three modes of the Spirit's presence and activity within the biblical narrative; namely, as "creation, re-creation, and final creation."[45] What emerges from this scriptural foundation is the claim that "the Spirit is the supremely mediational and relational symbol," insofar as all relations and mediations within God and without, start with the presence and activity of the Holy Spirit.[46] Yong is aware of the tendency to accuse various pneumatologies of falling victim to the subordination of Christ to the Spirit, which is why he gets in front of this accusation early on by explaining why his system is not subordinational.[47]

Yong's understanding of the relationality between the Spirit and the Son is dialectical[48] to the degree that "Word and Spirit" are "mutually defining as the 'two hands of the Father'"[49] and "respectively, the concreteness and dynamism of all things."[50] In short, the Word represents the "outer form" and the Spirit the "inner dynamic" of complex interrelationality.[51] By dialectical, then, Yong sees the Son and Spirit as co-determinate in identity and activity.

What emerges from this dialectical trinitarian theology with a pneumatological "starting point" is a pneumatological theology of religions that identifies the distinct economy of the Spirit in the world.[52] It is in this project that Yong highlights the critique of the *filioque* in that it tends to subordinate the activity of the Spirit to the Son in the realm of soteriology.[53] Yong's desire is to construct a pentecostal/pneumatological theology of religions that authenticates contextual varieties of engagements with the Spirit without resorting to Christological imperialism. Yong realizes that the hard and fast binary of general and special revelation breaks down if one integrates the influence of sociocultural contexts into knowledge and, therefore, theology. This means that the Spirit provides the contextual flexibility necessary for taking account of global experiences of the Spirit, whereas ending with the Son can oftentimes turn into imperialism by way of undermining—even extracting—social, cultural, and traditional inputs. The greater implication here is that the church itself is a cultural being, thereby not exempt from error.[54] Yong's point for a pneumatological theology of religions is that because the Spirit

42 *Chapter 2*

is universal, its expressions in human responses are going to vary, thereby inclusive of social, cultural, and traditional inputs.[55]

Universality, then, is understood by Yong in a critical sense. The foundational/metaphysical quality that undergirds the concept of universality in Yong's pneumatology contains within it a critique of Cartesian epistemological foundationalism. In contrast, Yong's definition of foundational is based upon a Peircean "postfoundationalist" epistemology that transitions out of a correspondence theory of truth and into a dialectical one between the knower and the known.[56] Yet, the universal *presence* of the Spirit remains, thereby undergirding the thrust and preservation of his version of foundational pneumatology and pneumatological imagination.

DIALECTICS

Yong distinguishes between the church and the World when describing the economies of Spirit and Word. Based upon Yong's early emphasis on constructing a pneumatological theology of religions that avoids the Christological impasse, that is, avoiding the reductively explicit and simplistic confession of Jesus as the Christ for the achievement of salvation, the Spirit is active in both church and World. Commenting on the complexity of confession within the church, Yong points out that "after all, Jesus himself warned that there will be those who will call him 'Lord' but do not know him since their lives do not bear the appropriate fruit."[57] In other words, an isolated dependence upon a logos Christology and explicit confession of Jesus as Lord as that which enables the discernment of the presence of the Spirit as well as salvation is misleading and obstructive. As an "intra-Christian matter," this approach ignores the reality that spiritual discernment as a phenomenological activity is inherently "processive, ambiguous, and dialectical" insofar as the variety of dimensions and intersections within the dialectic of form and content are in perpetual flux.[58] At every turn, Yong is attentive to this complexity of dynamic reality and personhood.[59]

Yong's foundational pneumatology commits to the reality of the Spirit as dialectically related to the Son; meaning, the Spirit is attributed with autonomy insofar as the Spirit is the "primary theological symbol for the presence and activity of God in the world"—scripturally, theologically, phenomenologically, and ontologically.[60] It is an extension of his interpretation and integration of C. S. Peirce's phenomenological categories of Firstness, Secondness, and Thirdness.[61] Firstness is the quality of something that acquires an abstract identity insofar as it is able to stand alone as a quality. For instance, taste, texture, smell, shape, size, and so on, all represent the quality of something. Secondness is the relational, or whatness, of that specific quality. In other words, qualities without relatedness remain isolated and stagnant. The size of an apple in relation to the size of a watermelon creates a relational disposition that includes the characteristics of difference and sameness within the existential experience of holding an apple. Thirdness, in contrast to Firstness and Secondness, contains the general character of relationality that mediates between Firstness and Secondness. It is the ground of relationality that gives birth to the process of moving from abstract possibility to concrete experience. Thirdness also acts as the "interpretant" of the whole process that thereby allows the rationality of Firstness, Secondness, and Thirdness to transpire and be known.[62] This phenomenological starting point opens into metaphysical and epistemological conclusions not as fundamental/totalitarian but as justification for a dialectical paradigm, consisting of phenomenology, epistemology, and ontology.

While a dialectical ontology has been growing in Yong's work from the very beginning, it gains a more explicit presentation in his second book, *Spirit-Word-Community*. Here, Yong engages the work of process thinkers Alfred North Whitehead and Charles Hartshorne, wherein he describes the significance of process philosophy as creating "a paradigm shift from the classical ontology of being to an ontology of becoming," which instantiates, according to Yong, "a *relational* metaphysic."[63] Yong endorses this shift, albeit critiquing the inherent nominalist quality of "the process of creativity itself" insofar as creativity exists as the assumed motor of movement within the two "poles" of "concrete actualities" and "abstract initial aims of the divine mind."[64] In other words, what is driving creativity in process philosophy? If "concrete actualities, arise and perish momentarily and are therefore unable, in and of themselves, to effect the dynamic of creativity, what drives the creative process onward?"[65] Given this lack of attention to the ontological hinge of creativity responsible for the passage from possibility to actuality, Yong notes that "it is therefore not surprising that nowhere in Whitehead's system is there an adequate explanation provided for just how creativity works to advance the interaction of the one and the many."[66] He is left with questions and doubts about the adequacy of process theology as it is.

Yong turns to modern and contemporary theologians who have reconceptualized the being of the Spirit as a force field that is the immanent relational structure (i.e., the bond of love) and economic relational structure (i.e., the two hands). The two dimensions that Yong preserves within this new arrangement are a relational, immanent, and economic trinity based upon the relational ontology of the Spirit. The Spirit is therefore that which is responsible for the creative passageway from possibility to actuality, from ideal to concrete. In the words of Yong,

in process terms, the Spirit is the creative field of activity which lures prehending entities toward their divinely appointed reasons for being. In [Walter]

44 *Chapter 2*

Wink's terms, the spiritual realm is that inner, dynamic realm of power and activity which drives reality's manifestations.[67]

The immediate implications of "creativity" reconceptualized within an ontology of becoming are the power of dialectic and the bolstering of divine transcendence.[68] The result from this explicit inclusion of the Spirit as the dialectical mediator/motor between possibility and actuality is the overcoming of "the dualism inherent in [Whitehead's] dipolar conceptualization" and concurrent movement toward a "triadic or truly relational metaphysic," that is, a trinitarian metaphysic.[69] Hence, it is Peirce that Yong ultimately sides with.[70]

TRANSCENDENCE

Yong's version of divine transcendence is influenced by the pneumatological imagination, offering "unique perspectives, sensibilities, and commitments"[71] and identifying divine presence and agency as being influenced by "an eschatological focus on what God intends to bring about."[72] In *The Spirit of Creation*, transcendence takes shape from the theology and science conversation to construct a "coherent" and "scientifically plausible" argument involving "miraculous divine action vis-à-vis the laws of nature."[73] To avoid baseless presuppositions, he critiques "popular pentecostal piety" that "uncritically accepts certain modernistic assumptions about the natural world" such as the "natural-supernatural distinction."[74] Here, again, we see Yong displaying a preference for nonduality wherein dialectic overcomes the "dipolarity" involved in "conceptualization" and "more suitably carries, connotes, and conveys the notion of transcendence than categories of spirit-matter and inside-outside."[75] A relational ontology supplied by a relational Spirit promotes transcendence as movement rather than dualistic assertion.

However, Yong maintains a critical disposition *against* nondualism to prevent the possible equivocation of divine action and human action, thereby losing the distinction between the finite and the infinite. In this context, Yong opposes co-creation because "God does not and cannot unilaterally act in the world," which is what Yong wants to preserve.[76] He prefers the "perlocutionary" quality of human participation in divine action insofar as human beings are responsive to the Spirit.[77] Thus, the concept of transcendence is reserved for a divine being who is not dependent upon the World thus qualified by classical versions of sovereignty and providence.

Yong's proposal regarding divine action is based upon an emergent system that consists of pneumatological, eschatological, and teleological coordinates.[78] Yong therefore enacts a "shift" in perspective "*from* origins *to* resurrection and eschatology," thus breaking out of an archaeological vantage point and into "a teleological perspective that identifies divine action only retroactively from a posture of faith, through the criterion of the coming kingdom that is manifest in the Son and illuminated by the Spirit."[79] Hence the "proleptic" character of divine action that is "by faith."[80] The heart of Yong's divine action theory—anchored in the work of Wolfhart Pannenberg and Ted Peters[81]—is an "emergentist cosmology" and "emergentist anthropology" insofar as Yong shifts from "divine action [that] has usually focused on the origins of the universe" into "eschatological thinking [that] looks ahead to the divine purposes regarding the end(s) of the world."[82] To this end, Yong also draws upon (1) the emergence theories of Nancey Murphy and Philip Clayton, (2) the quantum divine action theories (QDA) of Thomas Tracy, Nancey Murphy, and Robert John Russell, and (3) the chaos theories of John Polkinghorne and Arthur Peacocke.[83]

While Yong endorses emergence, he is sure to make one thing very clear: "for the record, I do *not* hold that God as spirit is also an emergent reality like human spirits."[84] In this sense, Yong endorses the quest for a "noninterventionist objective special divine action"; in short, belief that God does objectively act in the world without succumbing to the natural/supernatural bifurcation. It is a pneumatic-Christological eschatology (i.e., resurrection interpreted as the continual inauguration of the kingdom of God via the power of the Spirit) and a pneumatic-teleology (i.e., divine action fulfilling the promise of consummation via the power of the Spirit[85]) with a strong "pneumatological assist"[86] wherein an "experimentally identifiable causal joint" between a divine actor and its effect is no longer required.[87] The proleptic rendition of divine action by faith releases experimentation from its archaeological bindings and places it into teleological possibility.[88] Hence, the *noninterventionist*, that is, nondualistic, quality of divine action that is retained as pneumatological, eschatological, and teleological.[89]

Along these lines, Yong endorses the non-mediated quality of divine action wherein such things as "miraculous healing, the charismatic gifts of the Spirit, and divine answers to prayer" are possible.[90] This preserves divine action as being unilateral, avoids "classical notions of double agency," and the "concordance between divine and creaturely actions."[91] Nevertheless, Yong continues to play with the idea of complex, ontological participation wherein subjects and objects are involved in the co-constitution of being.[92]

Yong returns to C. S. Peirce in order to sublate the so-called laws of nature so that the modern bifurcation of natural versus supernatural is overcome by way of a "triadic and evolutionary metaphysics."[93] The goal of this engagement between Yong and Peirce is the construction of a "generalist teleology" that avoids the deterministic paradigm of classical theism wherein God is identified as a *supernatural* meddler who mechanically guides the divine

46   *Chapter 2*

goal of history to its ordained fulfillment in a heavy handed way.[94] Yong is clear to distance himself from a "classic teleology in the tradition of natural theology [that] insisted the final cause existed in the divine mind and thus carried the creation onward toward its fulfillment (usually articulated in theistic terms)."[95] Rather, natural laws are characterized as "evolutionary, developmental, and dynamic" insofar as laws are habitual products that emerge and take form through contingency and repetition amidst a chaotic environment.[96] The implication is that the Peircean teleology adheres to productive effects, that is, tendencies, within the evolutionary processes of natural development insofar as dialectics involve "chance and irregularity on the one hand and uniformity and regularity on the other," thus claiming that "habits or tendencies are what bring" regularity out of irregularity.[97] A Peircean ontology of natural laws is therefore dialectical in that contingencies and spontaneities become necessities over time; they are undetermined movements that repeat until turning into habits, which then become laws.[98]

Because of the dialectic of contingency and necessity, divine action is both recognizable and unrecognizable given the formation of new or unknown actions that, based upon emergence and chaos theories, retain the possibility of divine action without being labeled as dualistically interventionist. The natural-supernatural bifurcation no longer holds weight when the paradigm switches to a relational ontology that contains dialectical movements of formation, contradiction, rupture, and reformation. There is, then, a postfoundational epistemology interwoven insofar as subjective and objective certainties are no longer prized and sought to be proven; rather, there is a mystery that is attached to the divine being that can only be recognized through a hermeneutic of faith characterized by "pneumatic, charismatic, and eschatological" perspectives.[99] With this paradigmatic shift, the natural and the supernatural are reconnected "within the wider teleological framework of Christian eschatology."[100]

Following relationality, Yong places divine action within the "interpersonal and intersubjective sphere" wherein "human beings live and move in response to God's covenantal initiative."[101] Yong, however, is not an open theist in that he rejects the possibility that God's act of consummation could ever come to naught, for this would be "protological thinking" instead of "eschatological orientation."[102] While Yong positions divine action within a God-World relational ontology, the climactic events of creation and consummation remain attributed to God. If this distinction gets lost, Yong fears the result will be an "anemic eschatology" with God unable to "experience us in the depth of our existential subjectivities."[103] Yong prefers to speak of "God as future" because the "centrality of hope as a theological and existential category in the Pentecostal orientation toward the future" calls for a metaphysic that is able to support eschatological closure.[104]

Thus, the concepts of trinity, dialectic, and transcendence are at the heart of Yong's theology, making them essential locations of analysis and extension in the sublation of residual dualism. The mechanisms of foundational pneumatology, trialectical spiral, and pneumatological imagination are the connective tissues of such concepts, disclosing passageways into transformation. Put differently, the ways in which Yong conceptualizes trinity, dialectic, and transcendence fuel and are fueled by these mechanisms. Philosophical and theological systems must be assessed and transfigured continually in the network of conceptual and mechanical understandings.

NOTES

1. On the interdisciplinarity of theology, see: Yong, *Spirit-Word-Community*, Part II; Amos Yong, *Theology and Down Syndrome: Reimagining Disability in Late Modernity* (Waco: Baylor University Press, 2007), 12; Yong, *The Spirit of Creation*, 29, 35, 133; and Yong, *The Cosmic Breath*, xii–xiii.

2. Yong forcefully states, "There is no room for metaphysical dualism in any theology of the Holy Spirit informed by the Pentecostal-charismatic experience." Yong, *Discerning the Spirit(s)*, 175. He arrives at this conclusion after working through the brief argument for charismata as being understood as "natural endowments as well as symbolic windows into the Spirit's presence and activity in the world," therefore no longer "supernatural inbreaking[s] of the Spirit into the ecclesial order." Yong, *Discerning the Spirit(s)*, 175.

3. See Yong, *Spirit-Word-Community*, 197, 224. See also Yong, *Beyond the Impasse*, 21. Yong identifies the "radical alterity" of other religions here as well.

4. Yong, *Spirit-Word-Community*, 230.

5. Yong, *Discerning the Spirit(s)*, 233n15.

6. Yong, *Discerning the Spirit(s)*, 254.

7. Yong writes, "The world is therefore symbolic of the divine which we experience and interpret, always partially, by the presence and activity of (what we symbolize as) the Holy Spirit. . . . In light of the triadic structure of experience proffered by Peirce, we cannot but shy away from claims regarding direct, unmediated experiences of the divine. All religious experience is symbolically structured. Our experience of God takes place through an inferential perception of the Spirit's legal and habitual endowment of the world which enables human understanding. Our cognition is verbal, ritual or other symbolic expression of our experience of the world made possible by the Spirit." Yong, *Discerning the Spirit(s)*, 114–15.

8. Yong, *Discerning the Spirit(s)*, 68–9.

9. "Our experience of God takes place through an inferential perception of the Spirit's legal and habitual endowment of the world which enables human understanding. Our cognition is verbal, ritual or other symbolic expression of our experience of the world made possible by the Spirit." Yong, *Spirit-Word-Community*, 114–15.

10. Yong, *Spirit-Word-Community*, 14.

11. In the words of Yong, "[T]he content of theology narrowly construed concerns the topics of divinity and of ultimate reality. On the other hand, theology broadly

48 *Chapter 2*

understood concerns the totality of God and God's relationship to human selves and the world understood from the perspective of faith." Yong, *Spirit-Word-Community*, 2–3.

12. Yong, *Discerning the Spirit(s)*, 173.

13. Yong, *Discerning the Spirit(s)*, 173.

14. Yong, *Discerning the Spirit(s)*, 224; Yong, *The Spirit of Creation*, 163.

15. Yong, *Discerning the Spirit(s)*, 173; Yong, *The Spirit of Creation*, 60–1, 217.

16. Yong, *Discerning the Spirit(s)*, 173, 194; Yong, *Spirit-Word-Community*, 139ff.; Yong, *Beyond the Impasse*, 156–7, 160; Yong, *The Spirit Poured Out on All Flesh*, 163–4; Yong, *The Spirit of Creation*, 11, 35, 148–9.

17. Yong, *Discerning the Spirit(s)*, 173.

18. Yong, *Discerning the Spirit(s)*, 224, 224n3; Yong, *Spirit-Word Community*, 22–3, 230.

19. Yong, *The Spirit of Creation*, 142.

20. Yong, *Discerning the Spirit(s)*, 102, 102n5.

21. Yong, *Discerning the Spirit(s)*, 248.

22. Yong, *The Spirit of Creation*, 102.

23. Yong, *Beyond the Impasse*, 165.

24. Yong, *Discerning the Spirit(s)*, 63.

25. Yong, *Discerning the Spirit(s)*, 175. He arrives at this conclusion after working through the brief argument for charismata as "natural endowments as well as symbolic windows into the Spirit's presence and activity in the world," therefore no longer "supernatural inbreaking[s] of the Spirit into the ecclesial order." Yong, *Discerning the Spirit(s)*, 175.

26. In full, "Such an imagination provides us with a fundamental orientation to God, ourselves and the world, and renders more plausible the idea of God as present and active in the world. Further, this imagination serves as the foundation—albeit, as I will explain later, a 'shifting' one—for our philosophical theology of the Holy Spirit. The central component of this foundational pneumatology will be a trinitarian metaphysics of creation and a theology of symbolism formulated in dialogue with Charles S. Peirce, Robert Cummings Neville, and Donald Gelpi." Yong, *Discerning the Spirit(s)*, 29–30.

27. Yong, *Discerning the Spirit(s)*, 58.

28. For instance, Yong cautions against "the Holy Spirit becom[ing] the 'silent member' of the Trinity and pneumatology . . . subordinated to Christology." Yong, *Discerning the Spirit(s)*, 111.

29. Yong writes: "There is, on the one hand, a perichoretical relationality that is at the heart of the divine relation to the world: the economies of the Word and that of the Spirit are mutually related, and should not be subordinated either to the other. On the other hand, rather than being understood as being interdependent only upon each other and thus implying mutual definition, the divine missions should also be seen both as dimensionally affiliated and thus implying autonomy in relationality and vice versa, and as somehow commonly originating in the mystery of the Father." Yong, *Discerning the Spirit(s)*, 69.

30. Yong, *Discerning the Spirit(s)*, 70.

31. "the spirit of Jesus is also the spirit of God and these aspects of the Spirit's identity are both related and distinct. Certainly, this distinction-in-relationship cannot

involve internal contradictions so that to be the Spirit of one disallows being the Spirit of the other. Simultaneously, this relationship-in-distinction can open up to a complementarity so that the light of the spirit of Jesus can unveil or reveal the image of God." Yong, *The Dialogical Spirit,* 285–6.

32. Yong, *Spirit-Word-Community,* 107.

33. Yong, *The Spirit Poured Out on All Flesh,* 137.

34. Yong, *Spirit-Word-Community,* 25.

35. Yong, *Spirit-Word-Community,* 8. For a more detailed understanding of what Yong means by "metaphysical" when addressing what he means by spirit, see Yong, *Spirit-Word-Community,* 15.

36. For example, Yong, *Discerning the Spirit(s),* 61–2, 116, 174–5, 203, 226; Yong, *Spirit-Word-Community,* 71, 87, 139, 215, 220, 258; Yong, *Beyond the Impasse,* 43, 43n8, 139, 169; Yong, *The Spirit of Creation,* 209, 209n8. See also Irenaeus, *Against the Heresies* (New York: Paulist Press, 1992/2012), 4.20.1 and 5.28.4.

37. Yong, *Beyond the Impasse,* 139n12.

38. Like many pieces of his core system, Yong inherits the necessary and vital aspect of community from C. S. Peirce. See Yong, *Discerning the Spirit(s),* 113–14.

39. Yong, *Spirit-Word-Community,* 22.

40. Yong points out that his goal in *Spirit-Word-Community* is to demonstrate the "Spirit as relationality, as divine rationality, and as the power or dynamic of life" even though not "an exhaustive portrait for a biblical pneumatology." Yong, *Spirit-Word-Community,* 115. Earlier, he states that "the objective of Part One . . . is to set forth and defend a trinitarian metaphysics that is relational, realistic, and communal." Yong, *Spirit-Word-Community,* 25–6.

41. Yong, *Spirit-Word-Community,* 116.

42. Yong, *Spirit-Word-Community,* 88. Here, Yong is pulling from the work of Walter Wink.

43. Yong, *Spirit-Word-Community,* 258.

44. Yong commits to the "traditional doctrine of common grace: that human life and experience is dependent only on the prevenient presence and activity of God through the Holy Spirit, and that this should put us on the alert for possible experiences of the Spirit and alternative specifications of the pneumatological imagination outside of explicitly PC or even Christian contexts." Yong, "On Divine Presence and Divine Agency," 186.

45. Amos Yong, *Beyond the Impasse,* 36. This chapter is a revised edition of Amos Yong, "Discerning the Spirit(s) in the World of Religions: Toward a Pneumatological Theology of Religions," in *No Other Gods before Me? Evangelicals and the Challenge of World Religions,* ed. John G. Stackhouse (Grand Rapids, MI: Baker Academic, 2001), 37–61.

46. Yong, *Beyond the Impasse,* 42.

47. See Amos Yong, "The Turn to Pneumatology in Christian Theology of Religions: Conduit or Detour?" *Journal of Ecumenical Studies* 35:3–4 (1998): 453. Yong repeats this clarification when he writes that "certainly, at any number of levels, one can easily succumb to an idolatrous exaltation of the Spirit to the neglect or subordination of the Word, even as another can succumb to a misguided Jesusology apart

50   *Chapter 2*

from the Father or Spirit. However, I am convinced that serious theological reflection today has to capitalize on the relational and mediational resources of pneumatology rather than 'forget' the 'silent member' of the Trinity as previous generations have done." Yong, *Beyond the Impasse*, 42–3.

48. "All determinate things consist of both *logos* and *pneuma*, metaphysically understood—having both forms of concretions and dynamic vectoral trajectories. The *pneuma*, or spirit, of any 'thing' is the complex of habits, tendencies, and laws that shape, guide, and in some way manifest and/or determine its phenomenal or concrete behavior." Yong, *Beyond the Impasse*, 129–30. Yong later explicitly uses the phrase "dialectic of Word and Spirit" when discussing the hermeneutical approach to Word and Spirit. Yong, *Beyond the Impasse*, 139n12.

49. Amos Yong, *Beyond the Impasse*, 169. Elsewhere, "Apart from the inner dynamic of the Spirit, Jesus is not the Christ. Apart from the concrete form of the 'Word made flesh', the Spirit remains hidden, ambiguous, ineffectual, and ultimately irrelevant." Yong, *Beyond the Impasse*, 134–5.

50. Yong, *Beyond the Impasse*, 130. See also pages 134 and 160 for reiterations of this claim. A claim that was present in his first publication where he puts forth a "fundamental thesis that both Word and Spirit are constitutive elements of every thing, every experience." He demonstrates this claim in the following way: "Tongues-speech is a sign that the two hands of the Father are at work, albeit in different dimensions. While this can be parsed in different ways—i.e., Logos in the bodily expressions, Spirit in the emotive; or, Logos in the form of glossolalia, Spirit in its functions— these need not be dogmatically construed." Yong, *Discerning the Spirit(s)*, 174–75.

51. Yong, *Beyond the Impasse*, 136.

52. Yong is following Georg Khodr and the Eastern Orthodox emphasis upon the *oikonomia* of the Spirit. Yong, *Beyond the Impasse*, 169n5.

53. See Yong, *Beyond the Impasse*, chapter four. Yong critiques the Latin West's circumscription of salvation to the Logos and therefore the church as the visible body of Christ. What happens when the question of salvation is placed in a pneumatological paradigm? What new avenues are opened for identifying the salvific work of the Spirit in the world that, while dialectically related to the Son, nevertheless holds a unique perspective on such salvific possibilities?

54. As a precursor to the following chapters, the speculative interpretation of this all-encompassing presence of error is that error is that which constitutes knowledge and identity in the first place, that is, negativity in its positivity.

55. See Yong, *Beyond the Impasse*, 47–8.

56. See Yong, "The Demise of Foundationalism and the Retention of Truth," 563–88.

57. Yong, *Beyond the Impasse*, 169.

58. Yong, *Beyond the Impasse*, 170, 169.

59. Yong consistently uses the word "complex" to describe things and actions and then proceeds to jump into the frays of such complexity. For example, community "as complex networks of relationships interacting with and including others beyond their normally defined boundaries" (Yong, *Spirit-Word-Community*, 17); "complex interrelationality between the orders of knowing and being" (Yong,

Spirit-Word-Community, 77); "a complex task in part because we are dealing with [Peircean] Thirdness in all of its complexity" (Yong, *Spirit-Word-Community*, 183–4); "a complex undertaking" (Yong, *Discerning the Spirit(s)*, 80–1); "a complex interactive process" (Yong, *Spirit-Word-Community*, 255); "human religiousness in all its complexity" (Yong, *Beyond the Impasse*, 17); "complexity and precariousness of the conversation" (Yong, *Beyond the Impasse*, 68); "complex of habits, tendencies, and laws" (Yong, *Beyond the Impasse*, 129–30); "essential complex determinations of being of which all reality consists" (Yong, *Beyond the Impasse*, 134); "complex nexus of forces that reveal themselves in a variety of forms" (Yong, *Beyond the Impasse*, 151); "complex human constructions" (Yong, *Beyond the Impasse*, 165); "dynamic complexity of lived human religious experience" (Yong, *Beyond the Impasse*, 166); "complexity as events" (Yong, *Beyond the Impasse*, 179–80); "complex issues surrounding the relationship between Christ and the Spirit" (Yong, *The Spirit Poured Out On All Flesh*, 28); "complex and complicated process of relationships" (Yong, *The Spirit Poured Out on All Flesh*, 97); "complex question of Jesus" (Yong, *The Spirit Poured Out on All Flesh*, 110); "complex contexts" (Yong, *The Spirit Poured Out on All Flesh*, 212); "complexity out of chaos" (Yong, *The Spirit Poured Out on All Flesh*, 282); "complex systems of organization" (Yong, *The Spirit Poured Out on All Flesh*, 282); "political complexities" (Yong, *In the Days of Caesar*, 71); "complexities of the early Christian political self-understanding" (Yong, *In the Days of Caesar*, 103); "complex cosmology of spirits, principalities, and powers" (Yong, *In the Days of Caesar*, 134); "complex realities of human existence" (Yong, *In the Days of Caesar*, 280); "diasporic and complex nature of Jewish identity" (Yong, *In the Days of Caesar*, 337); "complex religious and political environments" (Yong, *The Spirit of Creation*, 52); "complexity . . . of human life" (Yong, *The Spirit of Creation*, 65); "doctrine of salvation in all of its complexity" (Yong, *Renewing Christian Theology*, 4).

60. Yong, *Beyond the Impasse*, 164.

61. Insofar as the foundational pneumatology describes the universal and therefore public aspect of the Spirit, Yong connects his pneumatological concepts of relationality, rationality, and dynamism with Peirce's categories of Firstness, Secondness, and Thirdness. See Yong, *Discerning the Spirit(s)*, 112; Yong, *Spirit-Word-Community*, 91–6.

62. See Yong, *Discerning the Spirit(s)*, 117; Yong, *Spirit-Word-Community*, 22, 93, 95, 156–71; Yong, *The Spirit Poured Out on All Flesh*, 288–9.

63. Yong, *Spirit-Word-Community*, 91 (emphasis added).

64. Yong, *Spirit-Word-Community*, 89–90.

65. Yong, *Spirit-Word-Community*, 89–90.

66. Yong, *Spirit-Word-Community*, 90.

67. Yong, *Spirit-Word-Community*, 90.

68. Dialectic overcomes "the rhetorical (if not essential) dipolarity inherent in the process conceptualization," which then "more suitably carries, connotes, and conveys the notion of transcendence than categories of spirit-matter and inside-outside on the other (cf. Pannenberg 1997)." Yong, *Spirit-Word-Community*, 91. In other words, a relational ontology that is supplied by a relational Spirit defines transcendence as

52 *Chapter 2*

movement rather than a dualistic assertion of spirit versus matter or inside versus outside.

69. Yong, *Spirit-Word-Community*, 91–2. This move of inclusion of the Spirit as "creativity" is recognized by Yong as merely the development of what was undeveloped by Whitehead et al.

70. Yong, *Spirit-Word-Community*, 93.

71. Yong, *The Spirit of Creation*, 131.

72. It must be noted that this inclusion of the eschatological nature of divine action is a central contribution from the eschatological-trinitarian theologians of the twentieth century. For instance, Wolfhart Pannenberg, Jürgen Moltmann, Eberhard Jüngel, Robert Jenson, and Ted Peters. Yong, *The Spirit of Creation*, 131.

73. Yong, *The Spirit of Creation*, 118.

74. Yong, *The Spirit of Creation*, 113–14, 72, 102.

75. Yong, *Spirit-Word-Community*, 91.

76. Yong, *Discerning the Spirit(s)*, 93.

77. Yong, *The Spirit of Creation*, 101.

78. Yong, *The Spirit of Creation*, 96ff.

79. Yong, *The Spirit of Creation*, 88–9.

80. Yong, *The Spirit of Creation*, 97–8.

81. Yong, *The Spirit of Creation*, 86–8.

82. Yong, *The Spirit of Creation*, 87.

83. In particular, Nancy Murphy's basic theological account of emergence theory (Yong, *The Spirit of Creation*, 60–2) and intent to make sense of special divine action (Yong, *The Spirit of Creation*, 92); Philip Clayton's insertion of the subjectivist perspective in response to the hard problem of consciousness (Yong, *The Spirit of Creation*, 63–4, 149ff.), "emergentist monism" (Yong, *The Spirit of Creation*, 144ff.), and weak supervenience (Yong, *The Spirit of Creation*, 148); Robert John Russell's preservation of transcendence (Yong, *The Spirit of Creation*, 83), critique of reified natural laws (Yong, *The Spirit of Creation*, 90), and pneumatological and eschatological characteristics (Yong, *The Spirit of Creation*, 90–1); and John Polkinghorne's "liturgy-assisted logic" (Yong, *The Spirit of Creation*, 85, 88, 92).

84. Yong, *The Spirit of Creation*, 71.

85. In Yong's words, this eschatological-teleology is "the qualitative nature of the future-made-present." Yong, *The Spirit of Creation*, 94n59. He goes on to note that he "learned" this from LeRon Shults's discussion of the Hegelian "absolute futurity." See Shults, *Reforming the Doctrine of God*, chapter seven.

86. Yong, *The Spirit of Creation*, 96.

87. Yong, *The Spirit of Creation*, 97–8.

88. "I summarize my proposal to rethink proleptically the notion of divine action in thoroughly pneumatological terms. What emerges on the other side is a teleological perspective that identifies divine action only retroactively from a posture of faith, through the criterion of the coming kingdom that is manifest in the Son and illuminated by the Spirit." Yong, *The Spirit of Creation*, 88–9. See also Yong, *The Spirit of Creation*, 97, 126–7.

89. As Yong writes, "we may not be able to identify the *how* of the Spirit's (energetic?) action in the world, so there is not much to be gained from insisting on

such occurring; hence, the noninterventionist aspect of NIOSDA is preserved. But we will still be able to specify, in faith, that the Spirit's action has made such and such a difference in the world (at least in terms of the input of information), and thus can affirm divine intervention in this eschatological sense. . . . [Therefore,] without a causal joint, any miraculous answer, healing, or other evidence of God's response can only be affirmed within the bigger picture of the coming kingdom." Yong, *The Spirit of Creation*, 98, 99–100.

90. Yong, *The Spirit of Creation*, 99.

91. Yong, *The Spirit of Creation*, 98n67. For a summary of what is at stake in the classical debate on causality, see Thomas Tracy, "God and Creatures Acting: The Idea of Double Agency," in *Creation and the God of Abraham*, eds. David Burrell, Carlo Cogliati, Janet Soskice, and William Stoeger (Cambridge: Cambridge University Press), 221–37.

92. Yong "assume[s] a kind of relational universe in which any strong demarcation between 'objective' and 'subjective' or between epistemology and ontology illegitimately bifurcates (usually based on modernist presuppositions) the participatory character of our being-in-the-world." Yong, *The Spirit of Creation*, 100.

93. Yong, *The Spirit of Creation*, 118.

94. Yong, *The Spirit of Creation*, 124n62. Regarding a non-deterministic, non-mechanical, developmental teleology—that is, a Peircean teleology—Yong throws up another critique of Aristotelian substance metaphysics: "Peirce's triadic metaphysics left room for God, but they attempted a fully naturalistic account through retrieval and rethinking of Aristotle's final causes. Where Aristotle presupposed *fixed and immutable essences*, Peirce suggests . . . processes tending toward general final states (7.471)." Yong, *The Spirit of Creation*, 124.

95. Yong, *The Spirit of Creation*, 123.

96. In other words, quantum indeterminacy. Yong, *The Spirit of Creation*, 79.

97. Yong, *The Spirit of Creation*, 120.

98. This Peircean ontology is like Catherine Malabou's plasticity insofar as such laws are formed and able to form, are open-ended and closed, are irregular and regular.

99. Yong, *The Spirit of Creation*, 129.

100. Yong, *The Spirit of Creation*, 130. The key, though, is to reconfigure the being of God within emergence and chaos theories. Divine being, therefore, is understood as a product of the dynamic processes within the Whole. In this sense, co-creation is implied by the emergentist paradigm; otherwise, latent dualism remains.

101. Yong, *The Spirit of Creation*, 130.

102. Yong, *The Spirit of Creation*, 130n84.

103. He goes on to say that a thorough nondualism "runs against the reverse intuition deriving from ecstatic religious experiences (like that claimed at times by Pentecostals and charismatics) that there is a direct encounter with transcendence (divinity) beyond the split between object and subject." Yong, *Discerning the Spirit(s)*, 93n38.

104. Yong, *Discerning the Spirit(s)*, 93n8.

Chapter 3

Žižek's Hegelian Dialectics

RENEWING DIALECTICS

The Hegelian bloodline that flows through Žižek's philosophy is the speculative dialectic wherein the epistemological gap is transposed as the ontological gap.[1] With the speculative extension of epistemology as ontology, the gap that appeared to inhibit connections is reinterpreted as that which connects because everything is marked by dissonance. The failure to grasp the essential content of things-in-themselves is thus normalized as inevitable, given the reality of ontological incompletion. What becomes impossible, then, is a "fully constituted positive totality" given the universal presence of constitutive absence.[2] Indeed, speculative dialectics affirms the presence of negativity as bearing the possibility for life and change.

The negativity that separates the subject from the object is thus identified as the negativity that touches all subjects and objects. Subjectivity and objectivity are, therefore, equally destabilized and brought into contact through the negative, ridding the ontological frame of essentialist dualism. What this means is that the so-called thing-in-itself is not a complete, stable object waiting to be grasped by the subject; rather, the thing-in-itself is just as incomplete as the subject, thus participating in the same dialectical movement of Becoming. Simply put, "far from denying us access to the Thing-in-itself, the antinomic or contradictory character of our experience of a Thing is what brings us into direct contact with it."[3] With epistemology as ontology, the dualistic frame of subject versus object turns into a dialectical frame of subject-object wherein identity formation, that is, the logic of subjectivity, is revealed as a continual process and product of *reciprocal determination* between subjects and objects, subjects and other subjects, and/or objects and other objects. The meta effect of epistemological failure as ontological

56   *Chapter 3*

incompleteness is the arrival of a complex ontology wherein *things* are only *things* in relation to other *things*.

Within the speculative mode of the dialectic, negativity is that which underwrites the transition from dualism to nondualism. The theory of substance that claims (1) the essence of a substance *precedes* its properties and attributes and (2) core of substance is solid and impassive, is transfigured into a complex schema of identity, difference, and negativity; for it is only by way of absolute negativity and its expression of contradiction that identities emerge. Without this universal presence of negativity, identity gets essentialized into a deterministic, substance dualism. The implication being, according to Stephen Houlgate, "what we initially understand to be simply the causal action of one thing on another, is in fact the combined activity of mechanical and chemical objects working together."[4] Otherwise, identity remains essentialized, deterministic, and dualistic.

In a paradoxical sense, the Hegelian identification of epistemology as ontology does not require conceptual additives; rather, it requires attention to the already present dynamics of conceptual movement, albeit looked at from a different perspective, that is, the critique is internal. Žižek calls this paradigmatic change of perspective the "parallax shift" wherein "what we arrived at *has always already been*."[5] For example, the concept of transcendence looks different when viewed from a nondualistic perspective. When it is realized that the dialectical flow of reality was already present in transcendence from the beginning, one does not claim to be adding anything new; rather, one claims to be seeing things clearly.

In a dense passage from *The Parallax View*, Žižek goes further by claiming that the ontological gap that is seen as inherent to reality in this parallax shift of perspective

> is no longer a difference between two positively existing objects, but a minimal difference which divides one and the same object from itself . . . [I]n contrast to a mere difference between objects, *the pure difference is itself an object.* Another name for the parallax gap is therefore *minimal difference*, a "pure" difference which cannot be grounded in positive substantial properties.[6]

The "pure" difference that is present within subjects and objects alike is now conceptualized as difference proper. The solution to the problem of epistemological failure, then, is failure itself insofar as we accept that reality has *already* failed, that is, that reality is *already* incomplete based upon the universal presence of difference (from negativity).

If this epistemological failure is chalked up to the difference between a finite human reality and an infinite divine reality, dualism remains. But because the goal is nondualism, a commitment to failure is required insofar as negativity exists prior to the emergence of identities.[7] For Žižek, "the movement from one stage to another is not that from one extreme, to the opposite extreme, and then to their higher unity; the second passage is, rather, simply the radicalization of the first."[8] Failure is ontological in the sense that negativity exists prior to the formation of identity; life is—and will always be—robustly incomplete.[9]

The Hegelian schema that Žižek repeats here is the dialectical transition from Understanding (*Vernunft*) to Reason (*Verstand*) wherein thought transitions out of merely critiquing the immediacy of givenness to the affirmation of complex identity in God-World relation(s). Theologically, it is the eschewal of "the excess baggage of a suprasensible irrational Beyond" and, consequently, the acceptance of subjectivity as a composition of finite and infinite realities.[10] This self-movement of the Concept (*Begriff*) is what grounds a speculative dialectic insofar as the force of negativity is that which cuts and unites. Clearly, transcendence within a speculative dialectic prohibits talk of separated realms or dimensions of existence because nondualism signifies immanence.

Attuned to Yong's core themes of trinity, dialectic, and transcendence, Žižek's trinitarian logic, speculative dialectic, and material transcendence catalyze the adjustment of Yong's system toward philosophical and theological coherence. Žižek claims that the being of God consists of the collectivity of believers and thus only exists as a relational substance. God does exist but only insofar as God involves the World; hence, the speculative/relational essence of God. Following this claim to its logical end, the *thingness* of God and the *thingness* of the World are reciprocally constituted insofar as the being of God is no longer an in-itself nor the external Cause of the World; rather, the being of God and the being of the World are reciprocally determined amidst the one and the same process of Becoming. That said, the theological lesson of this chapter to be fleshed out is that the traditional qualities of God—for example, sovereignty, impassibility, immutability, and so on—must be critically interrogated and revised for the sake of fully entering into a nondualistic ontology, thereby standing up to Yong's own truth criteria of *coherence* and *correspondence* as they relate to philosophy and theology.[11]

PROBLEM RESTATED

To be clear, the problem to be addressed in Yong's work, and why Žižek is helpful, is a substance dualism of the finite and the infinite, of the World and God. This dualism—at both explicit and implicit degrees—posits a substantial difference between these two identities as things-in-themselves—whether Yong would agree or not—thus preserving the concept of divine transcendence as self-enclosed Otherness. What we are leaving is an Otherness that is supported by a binary logic that is inherited from classical metaphysics wherein, theologically speaking, fundamental primacy is given to an all-powerful God who exists prior to, and irrespective of, the World.

In substance dualism, the World ultimately becomes arbitrary and/or superfluous as it stands in relation to God. If God is responsible for existence, communication, and the ability of the World to understand—as is implied by God as Cause—then human capacity and participation are ultimately relegated to dependence upon, and determination by, God. In reasonable effect, the World as a passive substance contributes nothing creative to the communication between God and the World and is therefore silent. The human being, in this frame of logic, is an ontological by-product bound to its reliance upon divine instantiation.[12]

The problem of substance dualism becomes even deadlier insofar as communication between God and World in a dualistic framework is impossible, and communication between the two becomes impossible given the chasm of ontological difference between them.[13] Each realm of existence consists of a history of "structures, categories, and concepts" that are "presupposed in the cognitive encounter" with everything, so if said histories are essentially and substantially different, then communication between them is struck down.[14] That is, unless there is an ontological point of contact, which would then require a logical premise that moves out of dualism and into nondualism.

Theologians who endorse the essential separation of finite and infinite try to solve this problem by using the Spirit and/or Word as that which makes communication and understanding possible. For instance, Yong believes human consciousness is tied to divine consciousness insofar as the Spirit causes human awareness of the divine.[15] In this sense, the Holy Spirit is identified as the mediator of communication in the two ways of (1) carrying communication from infinite to finite and (2) enlightening the finite. However, this remains dualistic since the infinite is mysteriously able to cross the ditch of solid, substantial difference.[16] Either ontological dualism is critically surpassed with an infinite-finite speculative dialectic thus allowing communication to be possible or ontological dualism is retained with its requisite disconnection of substances and communication.

Such dualism relies upon a reductive ontology wherein the substance of God is completely other than the substance of the World and can only be addressed by the incredible claim that God makes communication happen. At this point, the World's interpretation of God's communication would be thoroughly relative since no real access to the Other is granted, thus leaving the interpretive distance between the two entirely subjective. Theological language thus becomes an "ungrounded play of signs" wherein "every possibility of critical reflection and transformative practice [in response to God] disappears."[17] What must occur for communication to become possible is a change not in content but in form, which will enact the transition out of a binary system and into a dialectical one. Put differently, the logical frame itself must be critiqued and sublated by shifting into the speculative mode of the dialectic wherein substances and/or essences—including the finite and the infinite—are, again, rendered complex and relational. What is needed, then, is the change in perspective from reductive separation to complex relation.

There are three types of relationships and four stages to be mapped out in the trek toward nondualism. The three *types* of relationships are (1) Subject and Object, (2) Subject and Predicate, and (3) Thought and Being. The first has to do with the collective community, the second with personal identity, and the third with ontology. The four *stages* that exist within each *type* are (a) dualism with knowledge, (b) dualism without knowledge, (c) monism, and (d) dialectic. From a distance, each type of relationship has four settings. In the first *stage* (dualism with knowledge) of the first *type* of relationship (Subject and Object), the Subject and Object are separate, yet the Subject can directly understand the Object. In the second *stage* of the first *type*, the Subject and Object are separate, with the Subject *not* being able to directly understand the Object (dualism without knowledge). In the third *stage* of the first *type*, the Subject is inherently related to the Object *without* difference (monism); thus, Subject and Object collapse into sameness. Finally, in the fourth *stage* (dialectic) of the first *type*, the Subject is inherently related to the Object and can directly understand it insofar as both Subject and Object are connected by negativity. In the final stage, Subject and Object identify with one another through plasticity and dynamism.

In the first and second *stages*, an outdated metaphysics of "free-standing autonomous substances" is retained.[18] According to Hegel, "the presupposition of the older metaphysics was that of naïve belief . . . that thinking grasps what things are in-themselves, that things are what they genuinely are when they are [captured] in thought."[19] A classical substance metaphysics constructs a dualistic relationship of Subject and Object—and/or Subject and Predicate and Thought and Being—as separate entities wherein the former can or cannot see the latter.[20] In theological terms, God exists apart from the World whether the World can grasp God or not. Consequently, the ontological presence of negativity, difference, complexity, and relationality are unknown or disavowed.

In the history of Western philosophy, Immanuel Kant makes the notable distinction between "phenomena ('things for us') and noumena ('things in themselves'),"[21] that is, appearance and essence.[22] For Kant, thought does not interact directly with essence but with appearance, and immediacy is replaced with mediacy insofar as thought is able to know appearance but not essence.[23] Hence, the incomplete phenomena of appearance emerge as distinct from the

60   *Chapter 3*

complete essence of the thing-in-itself beyond the "kaleidoscopic multitude" of appearances.[24] Therefore, Kant's transcendental idealism never shirks the "confines of traditional ontology"[25] thus remaining bound to a logic structured by substance dualism.

In the third *stage*, substance dualism is resolved by collapsing Subject and Thought into Object and Being, respectively, without differentiation. Put theologically, monism is defined as God being the singular, primordial substance of all Being. Monism denies the reality of finite substance and any response of the World since there is no difference that exists either between or within substances. In effect, the World becomes God without distinction and communication/collaboration becomes a moot point. Consequently, stages one through three give rise to the impossibility of communication in the God-World relationship as they are premised upon ancient definitions of substance. In this sense, dualism and monism are two sides of the same coin wherein theology reifies the ontology of Being in otherness or sameness.[26]

The first three *stages* presuppose a dualistic substance metaphysic, be it God as separate from the World (dualism) or God *as* the World (monism). How is monism a dualistic substance ontology? The logical frame of monism separates *sameness* from *difference* and then puts substance into the former category of sameness without remainder; thus, dualism is plotted along the lines of sameness versus difference. In this sense, dualism and monism are two sides of the same coin wherein theology reifies the ontology of Being as either dualistic or monistic.[27] Overall, dualism understands infinite substance to be *other than* finite substance, whereas monism understands finite substance to be the *same as* infinite substance, therefore, the only real substance that exists.

Dualism assumes that substance exists in two separate states of being: infinite/immaterial or finite/material. In this setting, divine being is a substance that exists entirely by its own doing, free from potential change that might occur during ontological feedback from finite interaction. Divine nature is thereby a self-enclosed, static, impassive substance that is unaffected by predications and/or events. Both states of being—infinite and finite—are reductively defined in the two following ways: (1) infinite being is external to finite substance and (2) finite substance is the product of one-way causality, therefore predetermined and passive. In short, there is no creative capacity inherent to finite substance because it will only be what it already is due to finite substance being completely dependent upon infinite constitution.

Monism, on the other hand, assumes that substance exists in a single state, whether materialist-monist or idealist-monist. Due to the lack of inherent negativity within classical substance ontologies, monism is framed by the binary of likeness versus difference, thus unable to take account of internal difference. Therefore, all three *stages* run aground on the issue of communication, thus warranting a critical metaphysic that changes the onto-logical frame from reductive reification to complex relation. Indeed, Hegel contends that the duality of finite and infinite is a reduction to particulars, missing the relational dynamics therein.[28] Speculative dialectics, then, sublate a binary logic that maintains the static opposition between inert identities as well as the division of being into categorical oppositions of existence, for example, God versus World, supernatural versus natural, transcendent versus immanent, special versus general, and sacred versus profane.

LOGIC(S) OF ESSENCE

To better understand the problem at hand, substance dualism functions on three structural levels: the cosmic, macro, and/or micro. The *cosmic* signifies the distinction of infinite and finite substances, that is, God and World; the *macro* signifies the retention of isolated, self-sustaining substances within a community such as person versus person; the *micro* signifies subjectivity itself such as the immateriality and materiality of an individual person, for example, the (material) body and (immaterial) mind. All three assume that substances are essentially cut off from one another. Yong's logic of essence takes two different forms, depending on whether he is dealing with the divine or the human. There is a contradiction that exists between these two theories of essence insofar as Yong *does* move beyond substance dualism in finite relations but *does not* in finite-infinite relations. On the one hand, Yong claims that there is no "hard" substance that defines a person; rather, each person is a complex composition of relations.[29] On the other hand, God is a singular substance without any infinite-finite composition. God is thus radically other than the finite world, which is where his dualism crops up. Indeed, early on in his career, Yong has gone on record stating that what unites Pentecostals and charismatics is their mutual experience of God as "wholly Other" in the "confrontation with the beyond."[30] Yong's overarching theoretical frame houses a type of *mediated* dualism wherein it is the Spirit that exists as the source of communicative transfer from the dimension of the infinite to the dimension of the finite. Unfortunately, mediated dualism does not go far enough to be identified as nondualistic. Hence, we move forward with Žižek to articulate a consistent and cohesive logic of essence applied to both infinite and finite insofar as they are dialectically related.

To enter the complex relationality of speculative dialectics, thought moves past the popular theory of identity-in-difference by piercing into the surface and grabbing hold of contradiction in identity and difference.[31] The phrase identity-in-difference suggests that subjects exist in-themselves, albeit related to other subjects by way of difference. The problem here is that identities-in-themselves are not yet fully relational, not yet seen as being cut by negativity. The concept of difference needs to be placed not *in relation to* identity but *within* identity itself. Speculative relationality recognizes negativity as being inherent to all identities within the God-World network. As Žižek writes,

> Hegel has nothing to do with . . . a pseudo-Hegelian vision . . . of society as an organic harmonious Whole, within which each member asserts his or her "equality" with others through performing his or her particular duty, occupying his or her particular place, and thus contributing to the harmony of the Whole. For Hegel, on the contrary, the "transcendent world of formlessness" (in short: the Absolute) is at war with itself, which means that the (self-)destructive formlessness (the absolute, self-relating, negativity) must appear as such in the realm of finite reality—the point of Hegel's notion of the revolutionary Terror is precisely that it is a *necessary* moment in the deployment of freedom.[32]

True freedom is the release from external determination and the acceptance of essential emptiness in the sublation of "opposition to contradiction."[33] Due to the negative/non-substantial core of Being, it is the reflexive quality of negativity that drives the creative process of Becoming. Thus, negativity is that which hollows out the projected cores of identities that are in relation to other identities so that their essence is no longer singular but complex. Žižek calls this the Hegelian transition from "opposition to contradiction" wherein "the universal, common ground of the two opposites 'encounters itself' in its oppositional determination, i.e., in one of the terms of the opposition."[34] This universal is negativity, and the encountering of itself occurs through the process of self-reflexive negativity. For it is at the place of contradiction that the speculative aspect—that is, the reflexive aspect—of the infinite-finite composition is realized as infinite and finite bound together by negativity.

In pursuit of a nondualistic theory of substance, Žižek follows Hegel when working out his own logic of essence. What is essence if it does not subsist on its own behind the screen of appearance? Žižek will eventually arrive at the speculative answer wherein essence is not separate from appearance but *is* appearance. This is the only logical way to make sense of essence if we are going to enter a nondualistic ontology of complex substance wherein essence no longer exists in an entirely different dimension or realm. This return to immanence is the basis of the theological death of God as the "big Other." Nevertheless, one can immediately see the impact upon systematics; for instance, revelation as accessible notwithstanding qualities of difference, for example, special and general, but the theologian's escape into ontological otherness no longer makes sense.

In response to the question "what is essence?" Žižek does not answer outright; rather, he enters the conceptual flow of essence by beginning at the most basic entry point of "common-sense realism"[35] wherein essence is thought to be directly accessed by an inquiring Subject.[36] For instance, simply gazing upon the Object will make clear what the essence of the Object is without complication. The problem with this basic immediacy, however, is that a diverse array of interpretations plagues the conversation. This antagonistic plurality inspired Kant to distinguish between the appearance of the thing and the thing's essence, thus allowing the perceiving subject to experience the thing without knowing it. In response, Hegel critiques Kant for establishing a "bad infinity" or "spurious infinite" due to the inaccessibility of the thing-in-itself, thereby throwing subjects into the dizzying spirals of guesswork[37] that lead to "relativisms."[38] Without direct access, the subject is overridden by anxiety and despair due to the repeated failure of thought. What Hegel does is take a step back and reframe the problem, noticing that the solution is already present.

Because Hegel sees Kant struggling with the right problem without going far enough in his analysis, Žižek claims that Hegel is "more Kantian than Kant himself,"[39] that is, that Hegel "think[s] Kant through to the end."[40] The meaning is twofold: first, Hegel fully endorses Kant's transcendental imagination in that "pre-synthetic zero-ground elements" do not exist because "the synthetic activity of our mind is *always-already* at work, even in our most elementary contact with 'reality'."[41] Second, Hegel sees the epistemological gap that Kant identifies between phenomena and noumena as being present in both, thus ontological.[42] By this *formal* change in structure, Hegel short-circuits the ontological dualism of phenomena versus noumena by seeing negativity as that which runs through both; the appearance of the thing is just as split as the thing-in-itself. The cut of negativity thus dissolves the external realm of noumena/Object/Reason/Law/God by integrating it into the appearance.[43] It is through the subject's experience of the failure to grasp the thing-in-itself and the object's failure to be of its own making that contradiction is realized as inherent to subjectivity and objectivity alike.[44]

Within the speculative mode of dialectics, the thing-in-itself is reconceptualized by way of the *ontological inconsistency*, which Žižek points to with his pervasive use of Lacan's "*non*-All" (*pas tout*).[45] Adrian Johnston supports this interpretation when he states that Žižek "defines 'essence' as the 'self-fissure'/'self-rupture' of appearance" and the thing-in-itself as "the avatar/representative of the fact that phenomenal appearances can't be taken together to form a uniform whole, an organic cosmos, a being at one with itself."[46] Therein, Žižek follows the same Hegelian transition out of the Kantian dualism of a "two-worlds metaphysics"[47] by taking Kant to his logical end, which is the further realization of the intractable power of negativity as that which exists at the heart of all reality.[48] With this change in structure, the thing-in-itself is no longer posited as being in a state of stasis. In fact,

64   *Chapter 3*

it no longer exists at all; at least, not in a classical way. Rather, the concept of the thing-in-itself discloses the inherent work of negativity thereby causing a change in the structure insofar as subjects, objects, appearances, and essences are all bound to this logic of the *non*-All.[49] With epistemology as ontology, "our painful progress of knowledge, our confusions, our search for solutions . . . is already the innermost constituent of reality itself."[50] If God is Becoming, then it follows that God is incomplete and God and World are, at least conceptually, united in the fruitful void of incompletion, the crevasse of negativity.

Žižek often refers to the reflexivity of the negative as indicative of its positive function. Negativity does not merely disrupt conceptual stasis but also grounds conceptual formation insofar as negativity is the condition of movement and Becoming. In brief, it is impossible to make sense of anything positive without the presence of its negative contrast, for identification would be impossible amidst positive sameness. In this sense, the positive presence of negativity makes conceptual identification possible and thus grounds the logic of the *non*-All/incompleteness. Žižek explains this type of reflexivity as "the inclusion of the process of knowing itself into the known object."[51] In the sublation of dualism, then, the belief that there are two separate dimensions of existence (wherein the knower thinks that s/he can indirectly know the object) gives way to nondualism (wherein the knower realizes that they are involved in the constitution of the object itself). In sublating nondualism, fractured appearances reveal the essential truths of immanent, historical processes.

With this change in the formal structure—from dualism to nondualism—by way of self-reflexive negativity, that is, the negative turning in on itself, or the knower involved in the known, the problem contains its own solution. One now realizes that failure is at the heart of identity; hence, there is only ontological instability insofar as the completion/perfection of identity is impossible. Negativity, in a twisted way, thus unites the Subject and Object in the Hegelian frame of nondualistic instability. As such, "Kant's limitation lies not in his remaining within the confines of finite oppositions, in his inability to reach the Infinite, but, on the contrary, in his very search for a transcendent domain beyond the realm of finite oppositions."[52] As Žižek sums it up, "what appears to us as our inability to know the thing indicates a crack in the thing itself, so that our very failure to reach the full truth is the indicator of truth."[53]

SPECULATIVE DIALECTICS

Hegel delineates the three "moments," or "sides," of his overarching speculative logic: (1) "the Abstract side, or that of understanding," (2) "the Dialectical, or that of negative reason," and (3) "the Speculative, or that of positive reason."[54] The problem that Hegel addresses is the poverty of conceptualization insofar as Thought stops at either the first moment of Understanding or the second moment of Dialectic, not reaching the third moment of the Speculative. Akin to the initial experience of failure being accepted as part of the process, so it goes with Understanding as the first stage in movement toward Speculative reason.

The first moment of Understanding is necessary and important as it presents the power of the transcendental imagination to surgically dismember what had originally been thought to be a solid, essential state of being; it "separate[s] what naturally belongs together" within a substantial "organic unity" of immediacy.[55] Conceptualization, however, cannot remain at this first stage because the mode of observation is an abstraction wherein categories and concepts are isolated from their contextual determination. In Understanding, then, thought has not yet taken account of negativity.

The second moment of Dialectic occurs when negativity comes into light, that is, "the predicates of understanding" are seen as negations of themselves and the thing turns into its opposite.[56] For example, (too much) pleasure turning into pain, (one-sided) love turning into hate, and (overwhelming) comfort turning into oppression. At this dialectical stage, essential stability gives way to plastic instability, and conceptualization has moved out of isolation and reification.

The third moment of Speculative sees the dynamics of complex identities and relations, noticing something coming out of nothing.[57] For Hegel, "the Speculative stage, or stage of Positive Reason, apprehends the *unity* of terms (propositions) in their opposition—the *affirmative*, which is involved in their disintegration and in their transition."[58] The Speculative, or positive reason, is situated within a logic of *participation*. It is the shift from Being to Becoming insofar as ontology becomes dynamic. A Speculative ontology of Becoming integrates Being and non-Being into its flow. The result of the Speculative Dialectic, then, is an ontological "plasticity" wherein everything is in flux and has the potential to be related by way of negativity.[59]

Žižek takes this and proposes a speculative logic that fits within a contemporary nondualistic ontology.[60] Riffing on Ferdinand de Saussure's definition of identity as the interplay of differentiality, he goes on to claim that "the very absence of a feature can itself count as a feature,"[61] and absence "is the core feature of dialectics proper" with negativity being the "pure"[62] difference that highlights the "irreducible antagonism" persisting in the (absent) core of being.[63] Negativity disturbs the façade of a solid foundation and offers a more coherent understanding of inherent possibility insofar as negativity is the very "condition of possibility."[64] Put differently, negativity in the mode of "pure"[65] difference highlights the "irreducible antagonism" that persists as the negative core of identity.[66] Because negativity is the non-foundational foundation, identity is secondary in that identity first emerges out of the chaotic flux of contingencies and then reinterprets its past through this newly found identity as if it had always existed. Self-reflexive negativity, therefore, not only takes away but also gives anew; it takes away an eternal, solid foundation yet gives a more coherent understanding of historical identity within a dialectic of the material and immaterial.

Within the speculative mode of dialectics, negativity is the void that bolsters change; it is the funding abyss in Becoming that allows motion to occur, thereby "free[ing] us from the static substantialism of Aristotelian logic."[67] The caricature of Hegel's dialectic as thesis, antithesis, and synthesis misses the "absolute" awareness of the contingency and open-endedness of contradiction.[68] Again and again, Žižek points out that Hegel's so-called synthesis, that is, a third moment, is actually the recognition of the problem of inconsistency, which is realized in the passage from *thesis* to *antithesis*. The *synthesis*, then, is not the sublation into a stable reconciliation or harmonization of opposites between thesis and antithesis but the recognition of ontological inconsistency.[69] That negativity is already present in the position of thesis because every position in a nondualistic ontology will always-already be split, barred, cut, gaping, lacking, and so on. It just needs to be recognized.

By way of rhetorical questioning, Žižek queries—as he often does in order to push thought "along the way toward the [correct] position"[70]: "What if, for Hegel, the point is precisely not to 'resolve' antagonisms 'in reality,' but just to enact a parallax shift by means of which antagonisms are recognized 'as such' and thereby perceived in their 'positive' role?"[71] If one is asked what it means to be dialectical, then, it would be incorrect to respond with a straightforward, well-formulated answer. To do so would be to ignore the dynamism of the negative within differentiality. To be dialectical, in theory, is to start with where one is at, that is, to start with a given problem or question, considering its historical and cultural development. It takes note of what approaches, formulations, and applications have transpired in relation to that problem or idea while observing the ways in which concepts and ideas have progressed through a variety of transmutations. To be dialectical, then, is to begin where one is at while simultaneously moving forwards and backwards into specific lines of inquiry and information, allowing the various paths of conceptual flow to speak for themselves within the overarching place, problem, and/or question being addressed. According to Žižek, what we are talking about here is the "self-movement of the Notion," which encapsulates this dialectical flow of history, society, and culture.[72] The point is this: to be dialectical is to continually critique propositional reification; to be aware of how and why meaning occurs.

Given this ontology that consists of dynamic negativity, dialectics is not an *a priori* method of deduction used to analyze an already determined process

Žižek's Hegelian Dialectics 67

as if the one who gazes is not also being gazed upon. As Rex Butler makes clear, "the dialectic is a process without a subject, a process which revolves around a void or negativity."[73] This does not mean, however, that there is no Subject involved in dialectical logic; rather, the Subject emerges from and returns to this constant movement of negativity; the subject is a constellation of contingent events vis-à-vis motivations, intentions, and reflections wherein *"the subject's own activity is inscribed into reality."*[74] To be dialectical is to undermine the false oppositions within and between the Aristotelian "categories of being" and follow identity as it simultaneously emerges, twists, splits, and persists.[75]

SUBSTANCE AS SUBJECT

Žižek's "self-reflexive negativity" narrates the transition from (1) negativity as the inactive background of difference, that is, negativity "reduced to a self-mediation of the positive Absolute," to (2) negativity as constitutive of identity.[76] Within the circumscribed context of Subjectivity, Žižek fleshes out negativity in the following way:

> [W]hen we are forced to confront the power of negativity in its naked purity and are swallowed by it, the only way to go on is to realize that this negativity is the very core of our being, that the subject "is" the void of negativity. The core of my being is not some positive feature, but merely the capacity to mediate or negate all fixed determinations; it is not what I am, but the negative way I am able to relate to what(ever) I am.[77]

Hegel's self-reflexive negativity, also known as the negation of negation, is not a return to the self-enclosed substance from whence one initially departs but the recognition that substance is split, therefore always in flux. Everything is wounded insofar as both Subjects and Objects are cut by negativity. *The dialectical knife cuts both ways*, as it were. In Žižek's own words,

> [R]econciliation does not mean that the subject finally succeeds in appropriating the otherness which threatens its self-identity, mediating or internalizing (i.e., "sublating") it. Quite the contrary, Hegelian reconciliation contains a resigned note: one has to reconcile oneself with the excess of negativity as a positive ground or condition of our freedom, to recognize our own substance in what appears to be an obstacle.[78]

Once again, epistemology is ontology.

In *Tarrying with the Negative*, Žižek expounds upon the transition from negativity-as-immediate to negativity-as-speculative, wherein "the universal, common ground of the two opposites 'encounters itself' in its oppositional determination."[79] If the only function of difference is to provide contrast between substantial identities that exist in and of themselves, then difference is merely the neutral background of a dualistic logic of subjectivity. In such a flat opposition, there is no inherent relationality.

In exploring speculative negativity, Žižek uses Hegel's example of the father-son relationship. In opposition, the father is the father in relation to the son, and the son is the son in relation to the father, that is, negativity-as-difference; viz., the father is not the father without the son and the son is not the son without the father, which is the "simple opposition between two code-pendent terms."[80] Inherent contradiction manifests when the analysis focuses upon one of the particulars within the father-son relationship. For instance, to be a father means to contain an "antagonistic relationship between what I am 'for others' . . . and what I am 'in myself'."[81] The father is therefore irreducible to its relational identity of "for others" because the father, as an identity that contains a *for others* content and *for itself* void, requires the analysis to include the rise of subjectivity without reducing it to a relational network of inert substances. The *for itself* does not imply the presence of a substantial in-itself; rather, the subject's disjointed, internal core of negativity.[82] As Žižek goes on,

> I am not only "father," not only this particular determination, yet beyond these symbolic mandates I am nothing but the void which eludes them. . . . Outside my relations to the others I am nothing, I am only the cluster of these relations . . . but this very "nothing" is the nothing of pure self-relating: I am only what I am for the others, yet simultaneously I am the one who self-determines myself, i.e., who determines which network of relations to others will determine me. In other words, I am determined by the network of (symbolic) relations precisely and only insofar as I, qua void of self-relating, self-determine myself this way.[83]

Hence, to be a speculative subject is what Hegel means by substance as subject insofar as the complex substance that goes into the formation of subjectivity is inherently lacking, and for good reasons. Žižek claims that "to 'experience the substance as subject' means to grasp that the curtain of phenomena conceals above all the fact that there is nothing to conceal, and this 'nothing' behind the curtain is the subject."[84] Therefore, what one has to remember is that both essence and subjectivity are not self-transparent because there is no Self to be seen in the first place. Rather, it is negativity in the mode of contradiction that exists at the center of essence; thus, substance as subject contains the productive void of negativity. As Jean-Luc Nancy attests,

The Hegelian subject is not to be confused with subjectivity as a separate and one-sided agency for synthesizing representations, nor with subjectivity as the exclusive interiority of a personality. . . . In a word: the Hegelian subject is in no way the *self all to itself*. It is, to the contrary, and it is essentially, what (or the one who) dissolves all substance.[85]

To understand the speculative presence of negativity as contradiction within identity, it requires the logical movement out of two popular frames: (1) "the all-encompassing One which contains/mediates/sublates all differences" and (2) "the explosion of multitudes."[86] The most difficult one to get out of is the latter, wherein ontology is reduced to plurality. To realize the speculative dialectic and the ground of contradiction, we must begin not with sheer multiplicity but, like the father *for others* and the father *for itself*, with the primordial relationship of the One and the *not*-One.[87] Why? Because singularity, or the One, must be shown to be inherently contradictory/complex rather than a positive substance amidst the not yet speculative identity-in-difference. Here, identities have not yet been realized as incomplete in themselves.

To this end, Žižek fleshes out Hegel's oppositional determination in contrast to Kant's external reflection. For the latter, there is an unattainable beyond, the thing-in-itself, thereby leaving the gazer with external reflections upon the distorted appearances of a supposedly pristine yet unattainable essence of the thing. With Hegel, we move from the external reflection of identity-in-difference to oppositional determination wherein negativity and contradiction are realized as the absent core of substance. In the words of Žižek, it is when "the opposition between the One and its Outside is reflected back into the very identity of the One."[88] Therefore, the multitude of appearances is what the thing is; there is nothing in-itself beyond these appearances. By focusing upon the negativity within the multiplicity of appearances, we start the move from *oppositional determination* to *reflexive determination* insofar as "negativity encounters itself among its species."[89] In this way, pure negativity encounters itself among the negativity of essence, substance, and subjectivity, thus revealing its dynamic quality of birthing and sustaining movement by way of absence. This repeated movement of self-reflexive negativity within reflexive determination is that which keeps the sutured subject alive and open to change.[90]

Hence, in the movement beyond the dualism of God and World, one commits to the ontological premise that everything is negatively (de)centered and the essence of Essence is reflexive negativity insofar as "self-closure is a priori impossible."[91] The ontological openness and complexity made possible by negativity mean that essence is that which emerges and continuously changes based upon the activity that transpires in and around the Void.

70   *Chapter 3*

The ontology of the Void makes sense when "we pass from the *lost object to loss itself as an object*."[92] Such openness and complexity made possible by negativity is thus a *performative ontology* built upon "the recognition of some permanent pattern in the continuity of random change"[93] rather than a "metaphysics of presence."[94]

The lowest point of subjectivity, then, is not "between (the opposed meaning of) two signifiers" that are separated by an impassive negative space but "between the signifier which means something (determinate) and the 'empty' signifier which means meaning as such."[95] Absolute negativity becomes a signifier that embodies the Void responsible for the constant negative force that disrupts a classical substance metaphysic of isolated subjects. In this sense, the One is always-already split into two: into the One and the not-One.[96] For,

> the One is always already in excess with regard to itself, is itself the subversion of what it purports to achieve, and it is this tension internal to the One, this Two-ness which makes the One One and simultaneously dislocates it, which is the motor of the "dialectical process."[97]

Here, we see the key difference between Yong and Žižek on what, exactly, the driving force of the dialectic is. For Yong, it is the positive presence of the Spirit whereas for Žižek it is the presence of the negative. By moving into the Žižekian understanding, the Spirit is not necessarily dispensed with; rather, the Spirit is equally cut by negativity. In fact, it is only with the presence of the negative that a fully nondualistic God-World theology can appear. Because the presence and non-presence of subjectivity are never fully reconciled, the ontological *contradiction* within subjectivity is universal . . . even when it comes to the symbol/being of God.

Hegel begins this path toward the speculative mode of the negative as inherent to the One when he moves beyond the traditional opposition between the Subject as an in-itself and the Predicate as manifestation(s) of, or additions upon, a stable Subject. This is known as Hegel's "speculative sentence."[98] He begins this argument by stating that "the general nature of the judgement or proposition, which involves the distinction of Subject and Predicate, is destroyed by the speculative proposition, and the proposition of identity which the former becomes contains the counter-thrust against that subject-predicate relationship."[99] In other words, the subject passes into the predicate and the predicate passes into the subject, thus creating a dialectical counterthrust wherein the *universal* (Subject) passes into the *particular* (Predicate), thus becoming an *individual* (Subject-Predicate).[100] In this last stage, thought "loses the firm objective basis it had in the subject when, in the predicate, it does not return to itself, but into the subject of the content."[101] According to Catherine Malabou, "the substance withdraws from itself in order to enter into the particularity of its content. Through this movement of self-negation substance will posit itself as subject."[102]

Specificity is needed to sublate the latent belief that the Subject is a stable substance in relation to Predication. To do this, thought must expound upon the speculative notion of the One and the not-One that is already at work in the position of the Subject. That is, there is already negativity and movement in the position of the Subject prior to Predication. What this means is that "there is no One at the beginning, every One is a return-to-itself from the two. The One to which one returns is constituted through return, so it is not that One splits into two—One is a Two of which one part is nothing."[103] Hence, it is only through the retroactive movement of the negative within the Subject-Predicate position that the Subject can be made sense of because the Subject never actually existed prior to predication; the Subject emerges.

The Subject, in the speculative sense, then, is virtual. What does exist in the virtual position of the subject is the ontological antagonism of the One and not-One insofar as "the One only becomes One . . . by acquiring a minimal distance towards itself."[104] Therefore, the Subject does not return to its starting point after passing into the Predicate because there is no actual starting point; rather, the Subject is itself constituted in and through the movement of self-reflexive negativity.[105] Prior to predication, the Subject is Void. As Žižek states, within the speculative dialectic the Subject is "a predicate-becoming-subject, a passive screen asserting itself as a First Principle, i.e., something posited which retroactively posits its presuppositions."[106] What is found here in this Subject-Predicate movement is that the Subject retroactively fills in the Void with whatever constituents it acquires in the many "derailments" of the Subject-Predicate movement. In short, the *starting position* of the "substance as subject" is a virtual one that can only be reached by way of retroactive conceptualization amidst the concrete particularizations within the Subject-Predicate position, just like the "owl of Minerva [that] begins its flight only with the onset of dusk."[107]

Thus, Žižek's Hegelian move is one from *external representation* to *reflexive determination* in the speculative sentence, which is clarified by the distinction between the immediate way of Understanding (*Verstand*) and the speculative way of Reason (*Vernunft*). Understanding assumes the Subject of the sentence to be an entirely positive substance that is simply predicated upon without any ontological change to the subject in-itself. In this non-dialectical frame of subject and predicate there is, speculatively speaking, not yet any determinate content of the Subject therefore the Subject—however framed—remains positively abstract/empty. Reason, with its speculative dialectic, however, disrupts the supposed stability of the sentence by following the initial binary of subject and *non*-subject in the Subject position as it passes into the Predicate position thus demonstrating the proper move into concrete particularization; the *subject* gathers *substance* only within so-called predication. What was thought to be stable is now observed as ontologically unstable and therefore repetitive. As Frank Ruda points out, "there is only a subject in repetition and in a strange way sublation."[108] Subjective identity is generated in the repetitive process of differentiation within the passing of the Subject and non-Subject into the Subject-Predicate dynamic. The inherent negativity of essence is, paradoxically, that which makes subjectivity possible even though self-reflexive negativity is only able to be registered retroactively.

Self-reflexive negativity is the speculative truth of the dialectic insofar as "this negativity, this unbearable discord, coincides with subjectivity itself" and "is the only way to make present and 'palpable' the utmost—that is, self-referential—negativity which characterizes spiritual subjectivity."[109] The incompatibility of the Subject with itself, that is, the failure of Subjectivity, is that which opens up the space for spiritual subjectivity. For the *spiritual* sense of Self is that which extends beyond a reductive materialism insofar as self-determination and self-differentiation result. In this sense, the speculative dialectic does not do away with *difference*; rather, it saturates it. And yet, the misunderstanding of the Hegelian dialectical process as a reductive totalization persists

Todd McGowan argues that the reason for the perpetual caricature of Hegel's speculative dialectic as totalizing is the inability of thought to recognize the positive quality of contradiction that exists in the position of the Subject of the speculative sentence. Contradiction is not a transcendental *a priori* category but the consistent failure of thought in trying to keep concepts and propositions isolated and stable.[110] Contradiction is therefore not a problem to be overcome but a manifestation of the ontological essence of negativity that is inherent to identity itself. Simply put, "all things in themselves are contradictory."[111] This, however, should be supplemented with, I would argue, the most potent section in the *Phenomenology*:

> The life of Spirit is not the life that shrinks from death and keeps itself untouched by devastation, but rather the life that endures it and maintains itself in it. It wins its truth only when, in utter dismemberment, it finds itself. . . . Spirit is this power only by looking the negative in the face, and tarrying with it.[112]

Within the speculative dialectic (1) the negative/deconstructive capacity of reason is that it tears formal stability apart and (2) the positive/constructive capacity of reason is that it retains the inherent relation between concepts and categories insofar as their composite identities are formed, deformed, and reformed through repetition.

The "motor" of the dialectic, then, is negativity not teleology.[113] And the *speculative* mode of the dialectic is the self-reflexive capacity of negativity;

Žižek's Hegelian Dialectics 73

the inherent void of identity that maintains both possible and actual identity formations. Therefore, contrary to popular opinion, what is *not* offered by the dialectic is a reconciliation of antithetical terms by way of a positively based mutuality wherein difference simply adjoins the conflicting terms across the neutral gap of difference. Within the speculative dialectical mode of being, difference is recognized as such thereby displaying its ontological capacity insofar as negativity remains in continuous motion *qua* non-presence or non-substantiality. In short, difference as such is not that which separates two distinct concepts and/or identities but that which separates each concept and/or identity within itself; it is the *noncoincidence* inherent to the One.

In summary, with this emphasis upon negativity within binary logic, no positive content has been identified or added; rather, the logical movements of (1) negativity as self-reflexive and (2) conceptual understanding as retroactive are extensions of negativity as immanent, thus forcing a change of perspective wherein the problem contains its own solution. Disturbance is primordial, and the experience of stability is an illusion created by the symbolic network that is constructed amidst the Void. Hence, the speculative dialectic is one that demonstrates the "non-All" of the Whole.[114]

NOTES

1. This theme is identified early on in Žižek's corpus and continues to make its mark throughout. The earliest explicit reference to this Hegelian transposition of the Kantian gap (that I am aware of) shows up in *The Ticklish Subject* where Žižek identifies the "pre-ontological dimension" of the Real, which continuously disrupts the "ontological edifice" of the Symbolic-Real. Žižek, *The Ticklish Subject*, 55. This realization leads to negativity as the "fundamental feature of dialectical-materialist ontology." Žižek, *The Ticklish Subject*, 57. See also Slavoj Žižek, *Organs without Bodies: Deleuze and Consequences* (New York and London: Routledge, 2004), 53.

2. Žižek, *The Ticklish Subject*, 60.

3. Slavoj Žižek, *Organs without Bodies: Deleuze and Consequences* (New York and London: Routledge, 2004), 53.

4. Stephen Houlgate, "Substance, Causality, and the Question of Method in Hegel's Science of Logic," in *The Reception of Kant's Critical Philosophy: Fichte, Schelling, and Hegel*, ed. Sally Sedgwick (Cambridge: Cambridge University Press, 2000), 244.

5. Žižek, *The Sublime Object of Ideology*, 251 (emphasis original).

6. Žižek, *The Parallax View*, 18.

7. Žižek puts it this way: "all we have to do to arrive at the speculative truth of a proposition of Understanding is to comprise in its meaning our subjective position of enunciation: to realize that what we first take for our 'subjective' reaction to it—the sense of failure, incompatibility, discord—defines the thing itself. So, contrary to the expanded doxa, Hegel does not speak of a kind of esoteric 'private language':

74 Chapter 3

he speaks the same language as we all do, only more so." Žižek, *For They Know Not What They Do*, 138n19. On this dialectical transition from Understanding to Reason, see also: Žižek, *The Ticklish Subject*, 85–6; Žižek, *The Sublime Object of Ideology*, ix; Žižek, *Less Than Nothing*, 188, 280, 380; Slavoj Žižek, *The Most Sublime Hysteric: Hegel with Lacan,* trans. Thomas Scott-Railton (Cambridge, ENG and Malden, MA: Polity, 2014), 10–11.

8. Žižek, *The Ticklish Subject*, 71.

9. See Žižek, *For They Know Not What They Do*, 138n19. On this dialectical transition from Understanding to Reason, see also: Žižek, *The Ticklish Subject*, 85–6; Žižek, *The Sublime Object of Ideology*, ix; Žižek, *Less Than Nothing*, 188, 280, 380; Slavoj Žižek, *The Most Sublime Hysteric: Hegel with Lacan,* trans. Thomas Scott-Railton (Cambridge, ENG and Malden, MA: Polity, 2014), 10–11.

10. Žižek, *The Ticklish Subject*, 74.

11. Yong consistently identifies his own standards of truth as coherence, cohesiveness, and pragmatic. See Yong, *Discerning the Spirits*, 217; Yong, *Spirit-Word-Community*, 164; Yong, *Beyond the Impasse*, 54, 71; Yong, "On Divine Presence and Divine Agency," 179. See also Amos Yong, "Tongues of Fire in the Pentecostal Imagination: The Truth of Glossolalia in Light of R. C. Neville's Theory of Religious Symbolism," *Journal of Pentecostal Theology* 12 (April 1998): 42.

12. It must be noted that this type of substance dualism between God and the World is a product of the philosophical and conceptual propositions that were used to make sense of the instability of nature in relation to the stability of God. Hence, God as creator and the World as creature.

13. A similar point is made by Paul Tillich when he claims that if human beings were separate from the being of God then s/he "could not be aware of" the "infinite." Paul Tillich, *Systematic Theology, vol. II, Existence and the Christ* (Chicago: The University of Chicago Press, 1957), 9.

14. Paul Tillich, *Systematic Theology*, vol. I (Chicago: University of Chicago Press, 1973), 18–19.

15. "Our experience of God takes place through an inferential perception of the Spirit's legal and habitual endowment of the world which enables human understanding. Our cognition is verbal, ritual, or other symbolic expression of our experience of the world made possible by the Spirit." Yong, *Spirit-Word-Community*, 114–15.

16. A dualistic understanding of finite-infinite is incapable of being dialectical since the two are placed in ontological opposition. Žižek, *Less Than Nothing*, 112.

17. Taylor, *After God*, 59–60, 298.

18. Fredric Jameson, *Valences of the Dialectic* (London and New York: Verso, 2009), 17.

19. Hegel, *Encyclopaedia Logic*, §28Z.

20. Žižek, *The Most Sublime Hysteric*, 20.

21. Kelsey Wood, *Žižek: A Reader's Guide* (Hoboken, NJ: Wiley-Blackwell, 2012), 99.

22. Žižek uses the following sets: phenomena and noumena, phenomena and Thing-in-itself, and appearance and essence. All three indicate the relationship between accessibility and inaccessibility within a dualistic framework. What Žižek

does, by way of reflexivity, is demonstrate that the gap between the two should be understood as signified by the latter and therefore transposed into an immanent frame. Therefore, the "noumena," "Thing-in-itself," and "essence" all represent this ontological quality of inaccessibility thereby located within phenomena.

23. See Andrew Cutrofello, *Continental Philosophy: A Contemporary Introduction* (New York and London: Routledge, 2005), 1–9.

24. Adrian Johnston, *Žižek's Ontology: A Transcendental Materialist Theory of Subjectivity* (Chicago: Northwestern University Press, 2008), 142.

25. Žižek, *Less Than Nothing*, 281.

26. Taylor, *After God*, 297.

27. This line of thought is inherited from Mark C. Taylor. See Taylor, *After God*, 297ff.

28. Hegel, *The Encyclopedia Logic*, §95.

29. For examples of Yong broaching non-substance metaphysics and the relationality of all things, see Yong, *Spirit-Word-Community*, 86; Yong, *Discerning the Spirit(s)*, 120n27; Yong, *Spirit-Word-Community*, 79, 86, 177–8, 243; Yong, *The Spirit Poured Out on All Flesh*, 163–4; Yong, *The Spirit of Creation*, 118–19, 145, 178.

30. Amos Yong, "'Not Knowing Where the Spirit Blows . . .': On Envisioning a Pentecostal-Charismatic Theology of Religions," *Journal of Pentecostal Theology* 14 (April 1999): 96. Elsewhere, Yong dips into finite-infinite nondualism but ultimately pulls back. See Yong, *The Cosmic Breath*, 20, 49, 71, 94, 142, and 182; Amos Yong, *Pneumatology and the Buddhist-Christian Dialogue: Does the Spirit Blow through the Middle Way?* Studies in Systematic Theology 11. (Leiden: Brill, 2012), 39–43.

31. Žižek, *Tarrying with the Negative*, 130–4.

32. Slavoj Žižek, *The Puppet and the Dwarf: The Perverse Core of Christianity* (Cambridge and London: The MIT Press, 2003), 28.

33. Žižek, *Tarrying with the Negative*, 132.

34. Žižek, *Tarrying with the Negative*, 132.

35. Nancy, *Hegel*, 19.

36. In the context of this project, the terms Subject and Object are employed as the two placeholders within the discourse of relational difference, whether it be a binary logic of opposition or a dialectical logic of complexity and collaboration.

37. See Hegel, *The Encyclopedia Logic*, §93–95.

38. Nancy, *Hegel*, 14.

39. Žižek, 232. See also Žižek, *Less Than Nothing*, 281.

40. Žižek, *Organs without Bodies*, 45. In Hegel's words, it is the "carrying out to its conclusion the entire development." Hegel, *Science of Logic*, 21.

41. Žižek, *The Ticklish Subject*, 33.

42. Kelsey Wood locates Kant's vital contribution in relation to Descartes (Wood, *Žižek*, 99).

43. Of course, there is still a place in Žižek's theory for objects, reason, law, and God; however, they are on the verge of being critically transfigured within his own version of Hegelian dialectical materialism. To be a materialist is the only proper way to break free from metaphysical dualism. For, as Žižek states, "everything hinges here

76 *Chapter 3*

on where we put the accent: is—in the idealist option—the monstrosity of the chaotic aggregate of phenomena just the extreme of our imagination, which still fails to convey the proper noumenal dimension of the moral Law? Or—the materialist option—is it the other way round, and is the moral Law itself, in its very sublime quality, 'the last veil covering the monstrous', the (already minimally 'gentrified', domesticated) way we, finite subjects, are able to perceive (and endure) the unimaginable Thing?" Žižek, *The Ticklish Subject*, 41.

44. Žižek, *Less Than Nothing*, 282.

45. In *Less Than Nothing*, Žižek offers a succinct yet wide-reaching explanation of just how powerful the logic of the non-All is. See Žižek, *Less Than Nothing*, 925. Elsewhere, Žižek argues that Hegel's totality is akin to Lacan's non-All. Žižek, *The Parallax View*, 167.

46. Johnston, *Žižek's Ontology*, 142.

47. Johnston, *Žižek's Ontology*, 17.

48. Žižek articulates this inability of Kant to follow his own thought in Žižek, *Tarrying with the Negative*, 244n41.

49. Žižek writes, "We overcome phenomenality not by reaching beyond it, but by the experience of how there is nothing beyond it—how its beyond is precisely this Nothing of absolute negativity, of the utmost inadequacy of the appearance to its notion. The suprasensible essence is the 'appearance *qua* appearance'—that is, it is not enough to say that the appearance is never adequate to its essence, we must also add that *this 'essence' itself is nothing but the inadequacy of the appearance to itself*, to its notion (inadequacy which makes it '[just] an appearance')." Žižek, *The Sublime Object of Ideology*, 233–4.

50. Žižek, *Organs without Bodies*, 56. He goes on to say that "the fact that we cannot ever 'fully know' reality is thus not a sign of the limitation of our knowledge but the sign that reality itself is 'incomplete,' open, an actualization of the underlying virtual process of Becoming." Žižek, *Organs without Bodies*, 56.

51. Žižek, *Less Than Nothing*, 845n56.

52. Žižek, *Less Than Nothing*, 267.

53. Žižek, *Less Than Nothing*, 17. Žižek goes on to credit the fullness of this Hegelian insight to Catherine Malabou's *The Future of Hegel*. He also notes the tremendous impact of Rebecca Comay's, *Mourning Sickness: Hegel and the French Revolution* (Stanford: Stanford University Press, 2011). See Žižek, *Less Than Nothing*, 17n15.

54. Hegel, *The Encyclopaedia Logic*, §79.

55. Žižek, *The Ticklish Subject*, 31.

56. Hegel, *The Encyclopaedia Logic*, §81.

57. Žižek, *Less Than Nothing*, 582.

58. Hegel, *The Encyclopaedia Logic*, §82 (emphasis added).

59. Hegel, *Phenomenology of Spirit*, §64.

60. According to Žižek, binary logic employs negativity as maintaining the "harmonious tension between the two (opposing principles, etc.)" thus assuming a "domain of firm identities." In contrast, within a speculative dialectic, negativity exposes "the inner tension, the impossibility of self-coincidence, of the One itself."

This means that negativity within the speculative dialectic points to the irreducibility of identities within themselves, insofar as an identity contains within itself a negative gap which prevents internal coincidence. The negativity within the speculative dialectic does not do away with distinction; rather, it opens the internal inconsistency within identity thus displaying an ontology of displacement within not only Subjects but also the One. In other words, the One is already Many. Žižek, *Organs without Bodies*, 67.

61. Žižek, *Less Than Nothing*, 582 (emphasis added).

62. Žižek, *The Puppet and the Dwarf*, 24.

63. Slavoj Žižek, "The Descent of Transcendence into Immanence or, Deleuze as a Hegelian," in *Transcendence: Philosophy, Literature, and Theology Approach the Beyond*, ed. Regina Schwartz (New York and London: Routledge, 2004), 247.

64. Žižek, *Less Than Nothing*, 93.

65. In the words of Žižek, "This difference is 'pure' difference: not the difference between two positive entities, but difference 'as such'." Žižek, *The Puppet and the Dwarf*, 24.

66. Žižek, "The Descent of Transcendence into Immanence or, Deleuze as a Hegelian," 247.

67. Jameson, *The Hegel Variations*, 48. See also Žižek, *Less Than Nothing*, 583.

68. For more on the role of contradiction in the speculative mode of the dialectic, see Andrew Cole, *The Birth of Theory* (Chicago; London: The University of Chicago Press, 2014), 34; Findlay, *Hegel*, 63; Stephen Houlgate, "Essence, Reflexion, and Immediacy in Hegel's Science of Logic," in *A Companion to Hegel*, eds. Stephen Houlgate and Michael Bauer (Hoboken, NJ: Wiley-Blackwell, 2011), 152; Todd McGowan, "Hegel in Love," in *Can Philosophy Love? Reflections and Encounters*, eds. Cindy Zeiher and Todd McGowan (London and New York: Rowman and Littlefield, 2017), 4; Alain Badiou, *The Rational Kernel of the Hegelian Dialectic*, ed. and trans. Tzuchien Tho (Melbourne: Re.press, 2011), 27; Hodgson, *Hegel and Christian Theology*, 135; Dale Schlitt, *Hegel's Trinitarian Claim: A Critical Reflection* (Leiden; Boston: Brill, 1984), 17–18; and Sungsuk Susan Hahn, *Contradiction in Motion: Hegel's Organic Concept of Life and Value* (Ithaca and London: Cornell University Press, 2007).

69. See Žižek, *The Sublime Object of Ideology*, 242.

70. See Kotsko, *Žižek and Theology*, 12.

71. Žižek, *Less Than Nothing*, 403.

72. Žižek, *Organs without Bodies*, 50.

73. Wood, *Žižek*, 33. Another way of defining "the void," according to Žižek, is "being deprived of all substance." Žižek, *Less Than Nothing*, 132.

74. Žižek, "Dialectical Clarity versus the Misty Conceit of Paradox," 244.

75. This thought is inspired by Nicholas Adams's brief distinction between Hegel and Aristotle, as Hegel's "dialectic" which "undermines" the "false oppositions" within Aristotle's method of "deduction." Adams, *Eclipse of Grace*, 5.

76. Žižek, *Less Than Nothing*, 304.

77. Žižek, *Less Than Nothing*, 317.

78. Žižek, *Less Than Nothing*, 507.

78 *Chapter 3*

79. Žižek, *Tarrying with the Negative*, 132.

80. Žižek, *Tarrying with the Negative*, 131.

81. Žižek, *Tarrying with the Negative*, 131.

82. "In 'in-itself', the consciousness (of an object) is not yet fully realized, it remains a confused anticipation of itself; whereas in 'for-itself' consciousness is in a way already passed over, the full comprehension of the object is again blurred by the awareness of the subject's own activity that simultaneously renders possible and prevents access to the object." Slavoj Žižek, *Metastases of Enjoyment: Six Essays on Woman and Causality* (London; New York: Verso, 1994), 188–9.

83. Žižek, *Tarrying with the Negative*, 131–2 (emphasis added).

84. Žižek, *The Sublime Object of Ideology*, 223–4.

85. Nancy, *Hegel*, 4–5.

86. Žižek, *For They Know Not What They Do*, xxvi.

87. Žižek, *For They Know Not What They Do*, 52. For Žižek, this speculative ontological relationship is "not between two halves, but between Something and Nothing, between the One and the Void of its Place" wherein "the opposition between the One and its Outside is reflected back into the very identity of the One." Žižek, *For They Know Not What They Do*, 52.

88. Žižek, *For They Know Not What They Do*, xxvi.

89. Žižek, *Less Than Nothing*, 501.

90. Other terms for negativity that help to make sense of this claim are finitude and/or fracture. The finitude/fracture at the heart of identity—recognized only after the fact—is focused on, which, in effect, critically bypasses the reductive deconstructionist understanding of negativity as mere privation and/or destabilization. Negativity is not only responsible for critique; it is also responsible for construction. Akin to the oft-quoted words of Michael Bakunin: "The passion for destruction is a creative passion, too." Michael Bakunin, *Bakunin on Anarchy: Selected Works by the Activist-Founder of World Anarchism*. ed., trans. Sam Dolgoff (New York: Vintage Books, 1971), 57.

91. Žižek, *Less Than Nothing*, 845.

92. Žižek, *The Parallax View*, 62.

93. Žižek, *For They Know Not What They Do*, xix.

94. Žižek, *The Metastases of Enjoyment*, 190.

95. Žižek, *For They Know Not What They Do*, xx.

96. Žižek, *Less Than Nothing*, 588. See also Žižek, *For They Know Not What They Do*, xxvi, 52ff.

97. Žižek, *Less Than Nothing*, 853.

98. Hegel, *Phenomenology*, §61. Donald Phillip Verene expounds: "Thinking that apprehends the true as the whole and can thus produce a science of spirit requires a different sense of the proposition than that which attaches a subject to a predicate to state a particular truth. This requires what Hegel calls the 'speculative proposition' or 'speculative sentence'—*spekulativer Satz* (par. 61). The speculative sentence or what he also calls the 'philosophical proposition' (ibid.) is Hegel's special idea in the preface. It has within it the dialectical motion necessary to present consciousness as alive and self-developing through its determinate shapes to the organic whole of spirit

as 'absolute knowing'." Donald Phillip Verene, *Hegel's Absolute: An Introduction to Reading the Phenomenology of Spirit* (New York: State University of New York Press, 2007), 8.

99. Hegel, *Phenomenology*, §61.

100. As Žižek interprets it, this dialectical counterthrust of the "Hegelian speculative judgement" means that the "predicate 'passes over' into the subject." Žižek, *Less Than Nothing*, 216.

101. Hegel, *Phenomenology*, §62.

102. Catherine Malabou, *The Future of Hegel: Plasticity, Temporality and Dialectic* (London; New York: Routledge, 2005), 11.

103. Žižek, *Less Than Nothing*, 473.

104. Žižek, *Less Than Nothing*, 473–4.

105. Even if there was a place for the Subject to return to after reaching the Subject-Predicate position, it would immediately be broken back down to its basic constituents of the One and the *not*-One thus causing the movement to begin again.

106. Žižek, *Absolute Recoil*, 29.

107. G. W. F. Hegel, *Elements of the Philosophy of Right*, ed. Allen W. Wood, trans. H. B. Nisbet (Cambridge: Cambridge University Press, 1991), 23.

108. Frank Ruda, "Hegel, Resistance, and Release" (lecture, University College Dublin, Dublin, Ireland, June 27, 2014), https://www.youtube.com/watch?v=VzTvFaDpTCY.

109. Žižek, *The Sublime Object of Ideology*, 235. See also Žižek, *Tarrying with the Negative*, 130 and Žižek, *Less Than Nothing*, 629.

110. Todd McGowan, "The Necessity of an Absolute Misunderstanding: Why Hegel Has So Many Misreaders," in *Slavoj Žižek and Dialectical Materialism*, eds. Agon Hamza and Frank Ruda (London: Palgrave Macmillan, 2016), 43–56.

111. Hegel, *The Science of Logic*, 381.

112. Hegel, *Phenomenology*, §32. For commentary, see Žižek, *The Metastases of Enjoyment*, 189, 201.

113. Žižek, *The Ticklish Subject*, 55. See Žižek, *Less Than Nothing*, 492, 853. See also Kotsko, *Žižek and Theology*, 9.

114. Žižek, *The Parallax View*, 17.

Chapter 4

Žižek on Transcendence and Trinity vis-à-vis Dialectics

CRITICAL TRANSCENDENCE

This chapter continues to follow the claim that a nondualistic pentecostal theology requires a critical take on dialectics and becoming and that it is Slavoj Žižek who provides Yong with the means for such modification. The specific contribution of this chapter, then, is encapsulated in the following phrase: transcendence without transcendence,[1] that is, *relational* difference without *ontological* difference.[2] In other words, divine transcendence is no longer something that exists outside of, or apart from, the World but within it. In God-World nondualism, "the absolute immanence of transcendence" becomes the standard by which all concepts and categories are disrupted and defined, resulting in a "materialized transcendence" without the inhibitions of a vulgar materialism and/or fear of mysticism.[3] Transcendence, then, is "not abolished, but rendered accessible" to all things in a God-World network.[4]

To solve the problem of dualism in Yong's theology, his conceptualization of God must traverse the "death" of the big Other. Within Žižek's philosophical theology, the God of substance dualism "disintegrate[s]" rather than is simply transposed into immanence.[5] This event of death is not only necessary but relevant insofar as contemporary theologies claim "transcendence within immanence" yet retain the classical understanding of God as separate from, or other than, that which is immanent. Therefore, to espouse "transcendence within immanence" without critically redefining transcendence *as* nondualistic is just as problematic as holding dualistic assumptions and committing to dualistic premises. The concept of transcendence must be redefined in order for theology to exit dualism and enter "the absolute immanence of transcendence."[6] Indeed, the "substantial-transcendent God" must die for a nondualistic theology to be not only possible but also coherent.[7]

Yong's understanding of transcendence retains reference to the ontological otherness of God. Žižek disrupts this divine essentialization of transcendence by conceptualizing the finite and the infinite as fully co-determinate. In a way, he "materialize[s] transcendence" by fleshing out the speculative relationship of the material with the immaterial while consciously avoiding a reductive (i.e., vulgar) materialism.[8] For Žižek, there is no external transcendence, no supernatural beyond where the essential being of God is housed; rather, the conceptualization of transcendence within immanence means that the finite and the infinite emerge in and through the same process of Becoming. Transcendence, then, is "not abolished, but rendered accessible."[9] Indeed,

> Hegel "became Hegel" when he accepted that there is no Absolute *beyond* or *above* the reflexive oppositions and contradictions of the Finite—the Absolute is *nothing but* the movement of self-sublation of these finite determinations; it is not beyond reflection, but absolute reflection itself. Once Hegel gained this insight, the distinction between Logic and Metaphysics had to collapse: Logic itself had to be identified with "Metaphysics," with the philosophical science of the inherent categorial network that determines every conceivable form of reality.[10]

Within the speculative dialectic of transcendence as a dimension of immanence, one cannot shove the question of God into the parameters of an outdated metaphysic of presence wherein God either exists or does not exist. The better question is, "How might it be possible for a non-dualistic God to exist?"

It is only in the full-blown critiques of classical theories of substance and transcendence that consistent and coherent nondualism can emerge. To recite Athanasius and the Cappadocians on substance (*ousia*), threeness (*hypostases*), oneness of substance amidst threeness (*homoousios*), and the intermixture of threeness within oneness (*perichoresis*) is not enough. Yong agrees with this point and has gone on record critiquing any and all misinterpretations of patristic theology as being evidence for a substance metaphysic. As Yong himself recognizes, a critical reading of patristics vis-à-vis metaphysics is not a problem since "the Church Fathers were motivated primarily by soteriological rather than by metaphysical concerns."[11] Even if the church Fathers were promoting a particular version of classical metaphysics, there are differences in how the term "substance" is understood and employed between then and now. And because today's theologian cannot merely depend upon historical snapshots for sufficient grounding, thought must continue the critical work of theological interrogation and construction.

Maintaining that God is the exception to the rule of immanence actually undermines any and all nondualistic systems as it reintroduces the logical problem of ontological difference that the speculative mode of the dialectic reveals and resolves. John Krummel states the problem succinctly when he writes, "If the substance is transcendent to our knowing and judging acts, how does it come to be the object of our knowledge and the subject of our judgment?"[12] To say the connection is made possible by the positive activity of the Holy Spirit only shifts the dualistic problem of ontological division from God versus World to Spirit versus World and confusion remains. On the other hand, if the concept of God is understood as ontologically relational, dialectic, and dynamic, as Yong claims, dualistic division is overcome with nondualistic relation.

To be relational in the speculative mode of the dialectic requires *plasticity* wherein all things are material and immaterial, impassive and passive, shaping and being shaped. To be dialectically consistent, then, God is plastic, that is, actively shaping the World while being passively shaped by the World.[13] But even this does not go far enough since God is not something that exists in and of itself. Rather, in the same way that the position of Subject explodes into complexity, so it goes with God. A nondualistic theology must rethink who and what God is for coherence with philosophical Becoming.[14] To maintain that God is an exception to dialectical immanence is to undermine nondualism altogether.[15]

TRANSCENDENCE WITHOUT TRANSCENDENCE

Following the Lacanian motif that "truth arises from misrecognition," Žižek's conceptualization of transcendence emerges *after* the initially failed conceptualization of transcendence as external.[16] Transcendence as external fails insofar as the ontological and epistemological gaps created by substance dualism are unable to be crossed unless one resorts to positing the absurd, that is, choosing to escape the problem of ontological difference by claiming that the crossing of said difference is possible by way of an unknown.[17] Based upon this initial failure of transcendence as external, a second conceptualization occurs, which provides the opportunity to establish a coherent definition of transcendence in light of the non-Whole.

Transcendence as external is judged to be an illusion, a misperception that is caused by a gaping hole that resides at the "center" of all phenomena.[18] Because a subject cannot see or pinpoint the substantial essence that exists at the "center" of an object, the subject misperceives this failure as *prohibitive* rather than seeing this failure as *revelatory*. As prohibitive, the subject believes there to be content beyond one's grasp. As revelatory, the subject realizes that the inability to grasp the essential core of an object means that there is no core. Phenomena and objects are not positive entities in the

84   *Chapter 4*

classical sense—that is, not predetermined or positively given by this or that superagency—but fragmented by the insistent presence of negativity.[19] The experience of the epistemological gap is therefore not indicative of ontological difference but of ontological connection insofar as everything is joined through incompleteness. Meaning, there is no final moment of completion amidst the relational Whole; rather, there is an inexhaustible force of negativity that touches every aspect of the system, often described by Žižek as the "Void" or the "abyss of pure potentiality."[20]

The Void of "pure difference"—something Žižek claims Hegel is unable to think[21]—is the Real insofar as all Subjects and Objects are cut by negativity like a dialectical knife that not only cuts the object but also the hand that wields it, slicing through all essential reifications. Put differently, negativity "precedes the terms it differentiates," exposing everything to the painful possibility of failure[22] thus Becoming precedes Being.[23]

The significance of this "pure" presence of negativity is this: there is no positive (i.e., in-and-of-itself) beginning nor end; there is no/thing that exists outside of the *absolute* process of Becoming. With its negative force, it breaks open stable, determinate concepts from the inside, thus allowing the freedom of flow to take precedence over and against stagnation. It is only by way of the initial experience of the failure of Being that Becoming is identified as that which precedes Being. Even though one first encounters Being as positive in the Hegelian mode of immediacy, the façade of stability gives way to the primordial flux of negativity.[24] Because error is a passageway toward truth, the concept of retroactivity is a hallmark of speculative dialectics.[25]

This relationship of Becoming and Being vis-à-vis negativity, retroactivity, and dialectic is akin to the relationship of contingency and necessity insofar as contingency preexists necessity. Necessity is identified, retroactively, as the interpretive reflection upon various contingencies that came together in events. Thus, necessity is an interpretive stance that arises after the event itself has taken place. As commentary on this point, Žižek writes:

> the process of becoming is not in itself necessary, but is the *becoming* (the gradual contingent emergence) *of necessity itself*. This is also (among other things) what "to conceive substance as subject" means: the subject as the Void, the Nothingness of self-relating negativity, is the very *nihil* out of which every new figure emerges; in other words, every dialectical passage or reversal is a passage in which the new figure emerges *ex nihilo* and retroactively posits or creates its necessity.[26]

What emerges from the Void, or the unifying *cut of difference*, is a complex ontology of relationality wherein subjectivity and objectivity are no longer circumscribed by the blunt impasses of impermeable borders; rather, they are both participants in the Whole, thus revealing the cooperative nature of identity. In this respect, identity is complex; by way of negativity, the dialectic of the One and the not-One, or Being and not-Being, precedes Oneness or Being. Thus, Subjectivity and Objectivity are no longer separated by a dualistic qualitative difference but dialectically unified in the universal experience of the insisting negative, that is, negativity as such. Hence, Subjectivity and Objectivity are already joined together in the absolute process of Becoming. Put differently, it is because of the all-encompassing experience of negativity within identity formation that Subjectivity and Objectivity are related.

ABSOLUTE KNOWING

Absolute knowing is not a final state of being but the recognition of negativity as inherent to the ongoing movements of Becoming and involvement in the ongoing constructions of reality.[27] The Subject no longer fights against the all-encompassing *cut of difference* but accepts it.[28] Žižek, therefore, describes Hegelian "reconciliation" not as "the magical intervention of a *deus ex machina*" but as a change in perspective wherein "the subject endorses the loss" and "re-inscribes it as its triumph."[29] Negativity is identified as integral to the emergence of substance as subject. The epistemological frustrations of the subject are reflexively identified as symptoms of its own ontological instability. Which is why, for Žižek,

> this sudden recognition of how the very obstacle preventing us from reaching the Thing Itself enables us to identify directly with it (with the deadlock at its heart), defines the properly *Christian* form of identification: it is ultimately *identification with a failure*—and, consequently, since the object of identification is God, God Himself must be shown to fail.[30]

The way "divine failure" is being used here does not necessarily lead to the claim that God does not exist; rather, God does not exist as external to the World.[31] Or, to put it in familiar terms, God is not a big Other. To use Hegelian terminology, the death of God as the big Other signals the logical shift from Understanding to Reason.[32]

How toxic is the idea of God as a big Other? In *God in Pain*, Žižek critiques the popular belief that if God did *not* exist, then *anything* and everything would be permitted. He makes the point that it is the "sacred Cause" that is needed in order to legitimize violent acts, which, in turn, contradict the human element of empathy in the face of suffering.[33] Meaning, acts of violence are quite possibly done in the implicit name of God more often than not. In contrast, and in Reason, God is not this big Other or sacred Cause

86   *Chapter 4*

that justifies our own desires and actions. Rather, with the events of the incarnation and death of Christ wherein "God falls into his own creation," into the contingency of humanity, God is emptied of its big Other status.[34] It is God, not human beings, who makes the "Pascalian wager" insofar as the outcome of self-sacrifice is not a guaranteed success; in fact, it might be an utter failure.

> Christ's death marks the birth of the Holy Spirit, the community of believers linked by *agape*. . . . Everything now rests on them, without any guarantee from God or any other figure of the big Other—it is up to them to act like the Holy Spirit, practicing *agape*. . . . There is no guarantee of redemption-through-love: redemption is merely given as possible. We are thereby at the very core of Christianity: it is God himself who made a Pascalian wager. By dying on the cross, he made a risky gesture with no guaranteed final outcome. . . . Far from providing the conclusive dot on the "i," the divine act rather stands for the openness of a New Beginning, and it falls to humanity to live up to it, to decide its meaning, to make something of it.[35]

After the death of Jesus as God, God resurrects in the Holy Spirit or in the love of the community. Namely, in political love (*agape*) rather than erotic love (*eros*). For Žižek, the mantra of freedom is not "anything goes"; rather, it is human beings taking on the responsibility to create a new world after the destruction of a former one, both theoretically and practically. Hence, Žižek, like Kierkegaard, chooses Christ over Socrates because Christ embodies the unique Event of a new beginning. In this sense, the transcendence of God is immanent, and Christianity provides the transition from transcendence as external to transcendence as immanent by way of the death and resurrection of Jesus. Simply put, "the Christian God is not a transcendent God of limitations, but a God of immanent love—God, after all, is love, he is present when there is love between his followers."[36]

Discovery of the "true infinite" is only possible after one enters the Hegelian "way of despair," which is caused by the tragic loss of God as big Other.[37] The familiarity of classical conceptualizations gets shaken, and thought, theory, and meaning become disoriented. To move fully beyond a classical ontology premised upon dualistic conceptualizations, the way of despair is inevitable and requires courage and perseverance to keep pushing through.[38] This constellation of dialectics, negativity, immanence, true infinity, substance as subject, and absolute knowledge reveals "Becoming [as] the Truth of Being."[39] Indeed, a dynamic system that is inherently self-overcoming.

Hegel's dialectics do not prop up a totalizing system of teleological determination; it is a method that takes account of the contingencies that have coalesced into the necessary conditions of a particular Event within Becoming. With Žižek, logic follows the conceptual transitions from *universality* (indeterminate being) to *particularization* (alienated determination) to *individuality* (substance as subject) wherein essence is a "coming-to-be" through movement and concretization via Becoming.[40] In this speculative mode of dialectical logic, Truth is retroactively posited as reflection upon the movement from abstraction to concretion, and the Hegelian "substance as subject" supports the claim that "possibility already possesses a certain actuality *in its very capacity of possibility.*"[41] Therefore, Žižek refutes the accusation that Hegel is a historical determinist by explaining that "the universal notional form . . . remains marked by an irreducible stain of contingency."[42] Indeed, truth emerges in dialectics and only then is able to be (retroactively) posited as the necessary condition of truth. This point is acknowledged and embraced by Žižek when he writes that "the truth of a given moment" within the "*logic* of the Hegelian dialectical process" is that which "retroactively posits its own presuppositions."[43] One can now see how the speculative relationship in dialectics fits within Hegel's absolute knowledge. Žižek's Hegelian "dialectical materialism" is bound together by an ontology of Becoming, thus retaining the overall instability (i.e., freedom) of the world that is made possible/actual by way of absolute negativity. All is beautiful chaos.

Absolute knowledge, then, results in the dissolution of the immanent Trinity, that is, that which tends to fuel the theologian's dualistic desire. Transcendence without transcendence, then, is the dissolution of the immanent Trinity. Thus, because there is no essential beyond, the path toward truth is part of the truth itself and the finite realizes that it is already involved in the infinite. It is the letting go of the classical definition of God in search of a coherent and consistent nondualistic theology. Divine personality and agency are thus thrown into a critical reconfiguration . . . not thrown out! As Hegel rightfully posits, "What is a theology without the knowledge of God? Precisely what a philosophy is without that knowledge, sounding brass and a tinkling cymbal!"[44] A speculative knowledge of God is one that is capable of "tarrying with the negative."[45]

CHRISTIANITY AND THE TRINITY

There are at least three reasons why Žižek is drawn to Christianity. First, Žižek prefers Christian monotheism because it discloses "the gap in the Absolute itself, the gap which not only separates (the one) God from [itself], but is this God."[46] The problem with polytheism—and/or pluralism—is that it has the illusion of establishing a harmonious Whole wherein differences signify arbitrary distance between identities in an atomistic world. Contrary to the desire for balance, the Christian narrative emphasizes the primacy of disruption. For instance, God (e.g., the One) is itself fractured by the event

88   *Chapter 4*

of death. In other words, the logic of polytheism promotes optimism in the desire for a harmonious whole, failing to see the proper function of negativity in subjectivity and relations. Negativity is not the passive void that simply makes distinction possible; rather, it is the condition of possibility *and* actuality par excellence.

Second, from a dialectical perspective, the Christian narrative supports the critique of dualism in a variety of ways. One, via the interrelation of finite and infinite in Jesus as the Christ. Two, with the critical moment of Jesus facing the absence of external intervention when he cries out, "My God, my God, why have you forsaken me?" (Matt. 27:46). Rather than interpreting these words as a nod toward Psalms 22:1, Žižek sees the bitter truth of the Passion as a divine experience of doubt, God as wrapped up in the Becoming of the World, and the loss of guarantee. For Žižek, "God's manifestation in human history is part of his very essence," so belief in the classical God is fueled by the desire for certainty amidst uncertainty.[47] Put differently, Jesus experiences the failure in immanence, which means that there is no guarantee that the God-World relation will prevail over ruin.

Employing Hegel's triadic structure of Universal, Particular, Individual, Žižek locates the incarnation as the particular event of Jesus becoming the "vanishing mediator" in the transition from Universal to Individual.[48] Žižek's "unorthodox" theology can be summarized in the following way: the Father is the abstract universal idea, the Son is the concrete particularization of the universal idea, and the Spirit is the collective embodiment of the Universal-Particular dialectic in the Individual. Žižek is simply following the movement across the Hegelian forms: the *Universal* abstract God, the *Particular* immanent God-Human, and the *Individual* experience of the absolute negative amidst the whole process.[49] Hence, *"this negativity itself is the only true remaining universal force."*[50]

> This is why Christianity, precisely because of the Trinity, is the only true monotheism: the lesson of the Trinity is that God fully coincides with the gap between God and man, that God is the gap—this is Christ, not the God of beyond separated from man by such a gap, but the gap as such, the gap which simultaneously separates God from God and man from man.[51]

Žižek locates the Incarnation as the Particular insofar as Christ becomes the "vanishing mediator" in the transition from Universal to Individual.[52] The Incarnation, as the Particular event, is made possible not by the presence of a divine substance but by divine negation. Jesus *is* God who is crucified and resurrected, albeit in a unique way, insofar as the resurrection of Jesus becomes the symbol for political love. God the Father as the Universal empties/negates into God the Son as the Particular of Jesus Christ, who then experiences the crucifixion of negation. The resurrection symbolizes the participation of human beings in the life of God in that Individuals experience the universal power of negativity as expressed in the dialectic of the Universal and the Particular. Therefore, the Holy Spirit is not a substantial thing-in-itself but the Spirit of "the community of believers" vis-à-vis the Particularity of Jesus.[53] Eternal life is thus "given to all who believe in him and decide to 'live in Christ'," which is a "parallactic" move in perspective that defines eternity as commitment to the present.[54]

God exists in and through the immanent process of the non-Whole. Here, God repeatedly experiences and passes through the ontological wound of Becoming, a negativity that is responsible for identity and relationality. The speculative dialectical conclusion to be drawn from this logic is: "What we and the inaccessible Other share is the empty signifier that stands for that X which eludes both positions" and therefore unites the Subject and Object.[55] To be clear, this negativity of the divine is not a fabricated void that God creates but is always-already there, gaping in the God-World network like a divine crevice. It is the eruption of an excessive void that cuts through everything.

Returning, once again, to the Hegelian position of epistemology as ontology, Žižek endorses "transpos[ing] the tragic gap that separates the reflecting subject from pre-reflexive Being into this Being itself."[56] In turn, this gap, this intrusive splitting, is that which unites God and the World. This gap is expressed in the Particular life of Jesus insofar as the dual nature of human and divine: the distinction between the two natures is preserved yet united through the negative space between the two in what is otherwise known as *communicatio idiomatum*.

Third, Christianity embodies the necessity of taking responsibility for one's decisions in the realm of political life.[57] This combination of an ideological critique of harmony and transcendence, coupled with the insertion of political love, promotes the awareness and responsibility of thought and action in the world, that is, of a loving/revolutionary praxis. "Christianity is a 'religion of Love'" insofar as "one singles out, focuses on, a finite temporal object," that is, Christ, "which 'means more than anything else'," thereby causing a reordering of subjectivity and its entire existence.[58] By privileging the Christian message, a particular type of love emerges insofar as political immediacy takes precedence.[59]

Indeed, two recurring passages in Žižek's work to support this point are Matthew 10:34[60] and Luke 14:26.[61] Matthew 10:34 reads, "Do not think that I have come to bring peace to earth; I have not come to bring peace, but a sword" (NRSV). And Luke 14:26 reads, "Whoever comes to me and does not hate father and mother, wife and children, brothers and sisters, yes, even life itself, cannot be my disciple" (NRSV). "True love," therefore, "is precisely the opposite of *forsaking the promise of Eternity itself for an imperfect*

90   *Chapter 4*

individual."[62] True love becomes an exception insofar as it colors the entire worldview and affects our daily obligations. True love becomes "an Absolute [that] intervenes and derails the normal run of our affairs: it is not so much that the standard hierarchy of values is inverted, but, more radically, that another dimension enters the scene, a different level of being."[63] Regarding revolutionary potential, it is the violent love of Christ that calls us into subversive activity insofar as "Christianity . . . offers Christ as a mortal-temporal individual, and insists that belief in the *temporal* Event of Incarnation is the only path to *eternal* truth and salvation," and in this privileging of a temporal event *"change (undo the effects of) eternity itself."*[64]

ONLY THE ECONOMIC

Žižek moves beyond two reductive definitions of God: (1) God as *reducible* to the world and (2) God as *irreducible* to the world. The former collapses God into the community insofar as God is merely the human projection of the mind without any uniqueness of its own (i.e., metaphorical), whereas the latter detaches God from the community insofar as God exists in a supernatural beyond (i.e., literal). Žižek claims that both the metaphorical and literal definitions fall short of how the symbol of God functions within a speculative dialectic:

> It is, of course, not "literally" [that we define God] (we are materialists, there is no God), but it is also not "metaphorically" ("God" is not just a metaphor, a mystifying expression, of human passions, desires, ideals, etc.). What such a "metaphorical" reading misses is the dimension of the Inhuman as internal ("extimate") to being-human: "God" (the divine) is a name for that which in man is not human, for the inhuman core that sustains being-human.[65]

Elsewhere, Žižek writes,

> [O]f course there is no Spirit as a substantial entity above and beyond individuals but this does not make Hegel a nominalist—there is "something more" than the reality of individuals, and this "more" is the virtual Real which always supplements reality, "more than nothing, but less than something."[66]

What is this "something more" that Žižek is pointing toward? It is the combination of absolute negativity and the accompanying shift into speculative logic. And here is the place of reversal: "the love that bonds you, *is* the resurrected Christ!"[67]

God is, therefore, "ex-timate" insofar as God is the "non-assimilable foreign body in the very kernel of the subject."[68] God is that which is responsible for the conceptual decentering yet unification of all reality; it is the "inherent excess" of existence that "resists symbolization . . . appearing as a rupture, cut, gap, inconsistency, or impossibility."[69] Put differently, God is that which cannot be symbolized, the productive Void at the heart of any and all movement, "i.e., we do not relate to him, he IS this relating."[70] The truth of the Trinity, for Žižek, is not a literal truth wherein the essence of the Trinity is reduced to a surface reading of the text (and tradition); rather, it is a "truth [that] has the structure of a fiction."[71]

In his first monograph, *The Sublime Object of Ideology*, Žižek carries forward the Lacanian[72] insight that "fantasy is on the side of reality" insofar as it "gives consistency to what we call 'reality'."[73] Fantasy, though, is not a "dreamlike illusion" that needs to be cleared away in order to gain access to the Real.[74] Rather, fantasy/fiction is the symbolic narrative that weaves coherence amidst chaos. The complex tension amidst the primordial antagonism of One and not-One exists within the symbolic dimension, albeit as an "excess" that cannot be fully symbolized.[75] Reality carries "the fundamental, constitutive lack" of force and relation within the symbolic dimension of truth.[76] Talk of God, then, is just as real as everything else in our speculative/non-substance ontology. God is that which symbolizes negativity that brings renewal and/or new life.

The combination of (1) the death of God as the big Other, (2) personhood as multiplicity, and (3) God as the divine insistence on negativity leads thought out of the binary of the immanent versus the economic. If there is no longer a God-World duality and persons are multiplicities, then so it goes with God. Hence, Žižek argues for the prioritization of the economic over and against the immanent. In a response to John Milbank's emphasis upon the immanent, Žižek replies that

> it is the "economic" Trinity which is the truth, the true site, of Christianity, and the "immanent" Trinity is nothing but its "reification" into an independent process; more precisely, there is absolutely no gap between the "immanent" Trinity and the "economic" Trinity: what was going on in the earthly reality of Palestine two thousand years ago was *a process in the very heart of God himself*; there was (and is) no higher reality backing it up.[77]

Notice how Žižek says "no *higher* reality backing it up." He does not say that there is no power whatsoever. The possibility of a nondualistic power that "ex-sists" in accordance with the symbol of God is available and ready to go. The trinitarian distinction between the immanent (in-itself) and the economic (in the world) starts to blur.[78] To retain the immanent Trinity, therefore, is to retain dualism. For "the lesson of the Trinity is that God fully coincides with the gap between God and man, that God is the gap—this is Christ, not the God of beyond separated from man by such a gap, but the gap as such, the gap which simultaneously separates God from God and [human] from [human]."[79] Hence, the prioritization of the economic over and against the immanent is merely the reification of a projected desire.

In short, the symbol of God must be completely freed from all dualistic reifications. This is easy to say on the front end but extremely difficult to sustain. This move to immanence is difficult because it challenges classical understandings of omniscience, omnipotence, omnivalence, and so on. If we redefine divinity as being relational, historical, loving, empathetic, and transformational, then the categories mentioned above become loaded with problems that would need to be revised for the sake of coherence. When dealing with the religious narrative, there needs to be a critical reconceptualization of who and what God is. In this sense, thought interprets the Christian narrative/representations (i.e., *Vorstellungen*) in their original setting while simultaneously interrogating the funding philosophical concepts (i.e., *Begriffen*) in play. These conceptual changes will inevitably transform the meaning of the narrative in ways that do not undermine but cultivate. In this sense, it is the dialectical engagement with the biblical narratives that keeps scripture alive.

The concepts of transcendence and trinity must be reconfigured considering the speculative mode of the dialectic with the climactic moment of the death of God as the big Other. In the dynamic of Becoming, it is by way of negativity that ontology is conceptualized as relational. Because of the universal insistence on negativity, all substantial reifications of essence are cut open by the dialectical knife, that is, the productive void. Hence, Žižek's ontology of the non-All includes the activity of the negative as both deconstructive and constructive insofar as it participates in the many processes of Becoming.

All these insights are achieved through failure; otherwise, the dialectical flow of abstraction to concretization would not make sense. The theologian must realize that the path toward the immanent Trinity is doomed because it does not exist. The transition into this speculative truth is that God and the World are equal parts finite and infinite. It follows that the interpretation of the trinitarian narrative goes through critical reconfiguration toward nondualism. God no longer represents substantial persons but the narratival transition from transcendence to immanence in the death and resurrection of Jesus as the Christ. Based upon the all-inclusive mode of the economic Trinity and divine negativity, God is neither here nor there. Rather, God is the name that is given to the living absence that makes movement and relationality possible. God is that which encapsulates the meaning of life, death, and resurrection for the World. It is a name that has no name. It is the mystery of Becoming.

NOTES

1. The phrase is my own yet influenced by John Caputo's use and popularization of Derrida's phrase "religion without religion." John Caputo, *On Religion* (London and New York: Routledge, 2001), 11.

2. My use of "ontological difference," here, is shorthand for ontological dualism.

3. On "absolute immanence," see Žižek, *Less Than Nothing*, 197–98, 704n3. See also Slavoj Žižek, "Is it Still Possible to be a Hegelian Today?" in *The Speculative Turn: Continental Materialism and Realism*, eds. Levi Bryant, Nick Srnicek, and Graham Harman (Victoria: Re.press, 2011), 206. On "materialized transcendence," see Žižek, "The Fear of Four Words," 73. See also Patrice Haynes, *Immanent Transcendence: Reconfiguring Materialism in Continental Philosophy* (London; New York: Bloomsbury Academic, 2012), 1.

4. Slavoj Žižek, On *Belief* (London; New York: Routledge, 2001), 90. See also Žižek, *The Ticklish Subject*, 84.

5. Žižek, *Less Than Nothing*, 232.

6. Žižek, *Less Than Nothing*, 197–98; 704n3. This phrase was first published in Žižek, "Is it Still Possible to be a Hegelian Today?" 206.

7. Žižek, *Less Than Nothing*, 232.

8. The phrase "materialize transcendence" is from Patrice Haynes, who deals with this trend in continental philosophy. Patrice Haynes, *Immanent Transcendence: Reconfiguring Materialism in Continental Philosophy* (London and New York: Bloomsbury Academic, 2012), 1.

9. Slavoj Žižek, On *Belief* (London and New York: Routledge, 2001), 90.

10. Žižek, *The Ticklish Subject*, 84.

11. Yong, *Spirit-Word-Community*, 243.

12. Krummel is describing the problem that is being addressed by Nishida Kitarō. John Krummel, and Shigenori Nagatomo, *Place and Dialectic: Two Essays by Nishida Kitarō* (Oxford: Oxford University Press, 2012), 14.

13. According to Catherine Malabou, *plasticity* is defined as "a capacity to receive form and a capacity to produce form. It is this double signification which enables us to treat the adjective as itself a 'speculative word', in Hegel's special sense." Malabou, *The Future of Hegel*, 9.

14. See Žižek, *Less Than Nothing*, 274 for Žižek's emphasis on Becoming, and *Absolute Recoil*, 352 regarding the delineation of Being versus Becoming.

15. John Krummel reiterates the problem of dualism succinctly when he writes, "If the substance is transcendent to our knowing and judging acts, how does it come to be the object of our knowledge and the subject of our judgment?" Krummel is describing the problem that is being addressed by Kitarō, Krummel and Nagatomo, *Place and Dialectic*, 14.

16. Žižek, *The Sublime Object of Ideology*, 59–60.

17. For instance, by using a God of the Gaps theory wherein God, or the Holy Spirit in Yong's case, is responsible for solving a logical problem and/or contradiction.

94   *Chapter 4*

18. Žižek's use of "illusion" is indicative of his Hegelian critique of classical metaphysics insofar as "substance" is not essentially predetermined, nor is it something that becomes completed in-itself or in relation to others. Substance is now thought of in a speculative mode wherein the conceptual and material realities are interactive. Thoughts, ideas, flesh, and bone are all participating in the construction of various identities and subjectivities without hiding a suprasensible beyond. In this sense, one does not begin with immanence but with failed transcendence and then arrives at absolute immanence. Regarding immanence as secondary, see Žižek, *Organs without Bodies*, 61; Žižek, *The Parallax View*, 36.

19. Žižek, *Organs Without Bodies*, 60–1 (emphasis original). See also Slavoj Žižek, "The Descent of Transcendence into Immanence or, Deleuze as a Hegelian," 245. In one of Žižek's earliest books, "*Limitation precedes transcendence*: all that 'actually exists' is the field of phenomena and its limitation, whereas *das Ding* is nothing but a phantasm which, subsequently, fills out the void of the transcendental object." Žižek, *Tarrying with the Negative*, 37.

20. Kotsko, *Žižek and Theology*, 116–17.

21. Žižek, *Less Than Nothing*, 481–2.

22. By painful, I am referring to the initial experience that accompanies the realization that there is no guardian of truth that protects one's philosophical and/or theological worldview from failure/change. Žižek, *The Sublime Object of Ideology*, 59–60.

23. See Žižek, *Less Than Nothing* (274) for Žižek's emphasis on Becoming and *Absolute Recoil* (352) regarding his delineation of Becoming versus Being.

24. Regarding Hegel's immediacy, see chapter 4.

25. See Agon Hamza, "Going to One's Ground: Žižek's Dialectical Materialism," in *Slavoj Žižek and Dialectical Materialism*, eds. Agon Hamza and Frank Ruda (New York: Palgrave Macmillan, 2016), 165–66.

26. Žižek, *Less Than Nothing*, 231.

27. Žižek uses "absolute" in "absolute negativity" as relational, not totalizing. Žižek, *Less Than Nothing*, 459.

28. Žižek, *Absolute Recoil*, 244.

29. Žižek, *Less Than Nothing*, 204.

30. Žižek, *The Puppet and the Dwarf*, 89 (emphasis original).

31. Even though that is where Žižek ends up (or has always been).

32. "We pass from Understanding to Reason not when this analysis, or tearing apart, is overcome in a synthesis that brings us back to the wealth of reality, but when this power of 'tearing apart' is displaced from being 'merely in our mind' into things themselves, as their inherent power of negativity." Žižek, *The Sublime Object of Ideology*, ix.

33. Žižek, "Only a Suffering God Can Save Us," 45.

34. Žižek, "The Fear of Four Words," 50; Žižek, *Less Than Nothing*, 706.

35. Žižek, "Only a Suffering God Can Save Us," 38–40.

36. Žižek, "Only a Suffering God Can Save Us," 47.

37. Hegel, *Phenomenology*, §78. See also page 42.

38. This network of immanence, negativity, Becoming, transcendence, and the true infinite is woven together by Žižek. See Žižek, *Absolute Recoil*, 352.

39. Žižek, *Absolute Recoil*, 352.

40. Hegel, *Phenomenology*, §789.

41. Žižek, *Tarrying with the Negative*, 158 (emphasis added).

42. Slavoj Žižek, "Hegel and Shitting: The Idea's Constipation," in *Hegel and the Infinite: Religion, Politics, and Dialectic*, eds. Slavoj Žižek, Clayton Crockett, and Creston Davis (New York: Columbia University Press, 2011), 228.

43. Žižek, *Less Than Nothing*, 457 (emphasis added).

44. Hegel, "Reason and Religious Truth," 243.

45. Hegel, *Phenomenology of Spirit*, §32.

46. Žižek, *The Puppet and the Dwarf*, 24.

47. Žižek, "The Fear of Four Words," 32.

48. Slavoj Žižek, *Did Somebody Say Totalitarianism? Five Interventions in the (Mis)use of a Notion* (London and New York: Verso, 2001), 50. See also Žižek, "The Fear of Four Words," 29. Peter Hodgson provides helpful commentary in Peter Hodgson, "Editorial Introduction," in *Lectures on the Philosophy of Religion: One-Volume Edition: The Lectures of 1827*, G. W. F. Hegel, ed. Peter C. Hodgson (Berkeley, Los Angeles and London: University of California Press, 1988), 12–13.

49. Žižek explains the speculative dialectic of the Universal and Particular in the following way: "This reading of Hegel which locates the 'reconciliation' of the Universal and the Particular into the very splitting which cuts through them and thus unites them, also provides an answer to the eternal problem of solipsism and the possibility of communication (between different subjects or, at a more general level, between different cultures). . . . In other words, communication is rendered possible by the very feature which may seem to undermine most radically its possibility: I can communicate with the Other, I am 'open' to him (or it), precisely and only insofar as I am already in myself split, branded by 'repression'." Žižek, *Tarrying with the Negative*, 30–1. See also Žižek, *The Parallax View*, 10, 44.

50. Žižek, *The Parallax View*, 107 (emphasis original).

51. Žižek, *The Puppet and the Dwarf*, 24. He repeats this logical flow of thought more recently in *Less Than Nothing*, 99n31.

52. This statement follows the Hegelian syllogism of universal-particular-individual. Peter Hodgson, "Editorial Introduction," 12–13.

53. Žižek, "Dialectical Clarity Versus the Misty Conceit of Paradox," 292.

54. Žižek, "Dialectical Clarity Versus the Misty Conceit of Paradox," 292.

55. Slavoj Žižek and F. W. J. Schelling, *The Abyss of Freedom/Ages of the World* (Ann Arbor: The University of Michigan Press, 1997), 50–1. See also Žižek, *Tarrying with the Negative*, 30.

56. Žižek, *Less Than Nothing*, 15.

57. I'm using the term "political" here in the broadest sense possible, that is, taking responsibility for human actions and their effects on social and cultural dimensions.

58. Slavoj Žižek, *The Fragile Absolute: Or, Why Is the Christian Legacy Worth Fighting For?* (London and New York: Verso, 2000), 96–7.

59. "As every true Christian knows, love is the work of love—the hard and arduous work of repeated 'uncoupling' in which, again and again, we have to disengage

96 *Chapter 4*

ourselves from the inertia that constrains us to identify with the particular order we were born into." Žižek, The Fragile Absolute, 128–9.

60. Žižek, *The Parallax View*, 99; Žižek, "Dialectical Clarity versus the Misty Conceit of Paradox," 285, 292; Slavoj Žižek, "Christianity Against the Sacred," in *God in Pain: Inversions of Apocalypse*, eds. Slavoj Žižek and Boris Gunjević (New York: Seven Stories Press, 2012), 64; Žižek, *Less Than Nothing*, 107, 975; Slavoj Žižek, "Concluding Roundtable: St. Paul among the Historians and the Systematizers," in *St. Paul among the Philosophers*, eds. John Caputo and Linda Alcoff (Bloomington: Indiana University Press, 2009), 165.

61. Žižek, *The Parallax View*, 99; Žižek, "Concluding Roundtable," 165.

62. Žižek, *The Puppet and the Dwarf*, 13.

63. Žižek, *Less Than Nothing*, 33.

64. Žižek, *Did Somebody Say Totalitarianism*, 151–2. See also Žižek, *The Puppet and the Dwarf*, 32–3.

65. Žižek, "Dialectical Clarity versus the Misty Conceit of Paradox," 240.

66. Žižek, *Less Than Nothing*, 97.

67. Žižek, *Less Than Nothing*, 530–1.

68. Žižek, *The Ticklish Subject*, 45. This definition of "ex-timate" is pulled from Žižek, *The Abyss of Freedom*, 45, and repeated in Žižek, *Less Than Nothing*, 150.

69. Žižek, *Less Than Nothing*, 333, 874.

70. Slavoj Žižek, "Some Thoughts on Divine Ex-sistence," *Crisis & Critique* 2 no. 1 (2015): 32.

71. Žižek, *Less than Nothing*, 76. This idea was formulated in Žižek's first book when he writes, "What we call 'social reality' is in the last resort an ethical construction; it is supported by a certain *as if* (we act *as if* we believe in the almightiness of bureaucracy, *as if* the President incarnates the will of the People, *as if* the Party expresses the objective interest of the working class . . .). As soon as the belief (which, let us remind ourselves again, is definitely not to be conceived at a 'psychological' level: it is embodied, materialized, in the effective functioning of the social field) is lost, the very texture of the social field disintegrates." Žižek, *The Sublime Object of Ideology*, 34.

72. Žižek consistently notes that his two main influences are Hegel and Lacan. For example, see Žižek, *The Most Sublime Hysteric*, 1–5.

73. Žižek, *The Sublime Object of Ideology*, 43–4.

74. Žižek, *The Sublime Object of Ideology*, 45.

75. Žižek, *The Sublime Object of Ideology*, 43.

76. Žižek, *The Sublime Object of Ideology*, 54. Žižek claims that "the most subversive core of the Lacanian doctrine" is "that of the constitutive lack in the Other." Slavoj Žižek, *Interrogating the Real*, eds. Rex Butler and Scott Stephens (London and New York: Bloomsbury Academic, 2005), 38.

77. Žižek, "Dialectical Clarity versus the Misty Conceit of Paradox," 253–4.

78. Žižek, "Dialectical Clarity versus the Misty Conceit of Paradox," 253–4.

79. Žižek, *The Puppet and the Dwarf*, 24. See also, Žižek, *Less Than Nothing*, 99n31.

Chapter 5

A Speculative Modification of Amos Yong's Trinity, Dialectics, and Transcendence

Paul Ricoeur once lamented that "the period of mourning for the gods who have died is not yet over."[1] The gods that Ricoeur is referencing are the changeless superagents who exist apart from the material world yet are able to intervene at will. This type of god continues to haunt systematic theology and philosophy of religion, as evidenced by promotional and/or reactionary types of responses. For example, the first response from theologians is *promotional* insofar as one's understanding of God remains at the level of rhetorical hermeneutics, thereby never entering into the conceptual relationship between God and the World. Thus, the theologian defaults to *promoting* the classical idea that God exists outside of the world and freely acts upon it whenever he wills without consequence. The second response from philosophers is *reactionary* insofar as one is unable to tarry with the symbol of God *beyond* the classical notion of God as a detached transcendence and superagency; therefore, the thinker *reacts* to such an idea in a reductive way by throwing out the concept of God altogether.[2] What I am saying, and what Ricoeur is implying, is that whether we admit it or not, our interpretations of religious symbols and systems are always-already influenced by a particular type of metaphysic that is ingrained in, and dispersed by, culture, and we would do well to interrogate these assumptions in order to gain better clarity and coherence regarding *theological* truth claims. Especially if theology wants to move beyond the widespread conceptualization of God as an isolated, impassive, subsisting subject—be it endorsed or denied.

Hegel makes a relevant point in the *Encyclopedia* when he distinguishes between the *history* of philosophy and the *culture* of philosophy. Change in the *history* of philosophy might have no bearing upon the *culture* of philosophy. As an example, Hegel argues that a "pre-Kantian" or precritical metaphysic has been pronounced dead in the *history* of philosophy, yet continues

97

to exist in the *culture* of philosophy, creeping in the shadows of thought and whispering sweet nothings into the ears of religious sensibility.[3] This particular incoherence between the *history* and *culture* of philosophy is still an issue in theology. Hence, we have not yet fully laid to rest our idolatry of the gods and, therefore, are not yet able to fully reappropriate the symbol of God in a truly dialectical way. In agreement with Ricoeur, "idols must die—so that symbols may live."[4]

Focus returns to Amos Yong and the critical extension of his tripartite structure of Trinity, dialectics, and transcendence in light of Žižek's Hegelian dialectics. First and foremost, the understanding of divine personhood as external from the World goes through dialectical sublation. Following Yong's lead, thought goes beyond the "dichotomies between sacred and secular," "religion and politics," "Christianity and culture," and God and World.[5] But his version of dialectic preserves the traditional definitions of transcendence and immanence, missing the incoherence between them.[6] According to Yong, this approach demonstrates a "theological nondualism whereby God is neither merely immanent nor merely transcendent . . . and neither merely emergent nor merely purposive and personal."[7] Unfortunately, this remains dualistic insofar as the transcendent and personalist qualities of God remain tethered to a substance metaphysic wherein divine identity and personhood are externally closed off. Nondualism does not balance transcendence and immanence; rather, it disrupts them. What is needed is not a balancing of the two sides—that is, of transcendence and immanence—but a transition out of a classical frame altogether, thereby reconfiguring transcendence, immanence, personhood, and relationality. The need to find a balance becomes a non-issue because the concepts no longer have a dualistic base.

THE SPECULATIVE TRINITY

A speculative approach to trinitarian theology emphasizes the ontological presence of negativity within the Trinity insofar as the trinitarian dialectic of identity and difference is not all there is. What is missing is the presence of negativity and a speculative understanding of relationality wherein instability is at the heart of identity formation. God is wholly relational, thus reliant upon concrete particularities and determinations within the World. Hence, God is not God until the universal, abstract essence moves through determination in and through the World, providing opportunities for self-reflexivity in the ongoing Becoming of God.

Negativity, then, is the "heart" of (the) God(-World relation) since it is negativity that makes life and identity possible. Based upon the emergence theory of reality that has been proposed by Yong[8] (as well as Žižek albeit in a modified way), God is not God until the universal, abstract essence moves through the conceptual work of determination in the World, thus providing the moment of self-reflexivity in the Becoming of (the) God(-World). This does not mean that God exists prior to concrete determination, for this would retain the dualistic understanding of transcendence that we are trying to supersede. The point is that while God is irreducible to the World, it is dependent upon it.

The question about whether God or the World comes first no longer makes sense when it is realized that both emerge from the chaotic throes of contingency and coincidence. The sacrifice to be made here is the idea that God was a complete being prior to the God-World relationship, that is, a subject outside of the God-World network. This does not mean, however, that God is nothing prior to the World; rather, incomplete. To claim that one exists prior to the other—that one is reducible to itself—signifies the return to metaphysical dualism.

If one is no longer thinking in the traditional vein of substance metaphysics, divine essence must be reconceptualized accordingly. The speculative focuses on the inherent presence of negativity, dialectical flow, speculative relationality, and the ontological field of Becoming; all of which are already present yet unrealized within the traditional frame. Here, classical theories of substance now show up as complex and dynamic. What is meant by God in this speculative frame is going to be very different than what is meant in the traditional sense. Now, God is neither alive, dead, isolated, nor dispersed; rather, God is complex and dynamic. And God-World nonduality means that whatever happens in one involves the other in some way.[9] While the answer to the question, "What is God?" is neither simple nor straightforward, it is safe to initially say that God is dynamic, connected, and disruptive. The rest of the answer must unfold in time to demonstrate conceptual fluidity and the inability to reify who or what God is. Neither God nor World can be reified into propositional statements devoid of process.

My claim, then, is that God is alive but only in the speculative sense. The main difficulty for the theologian who tries to thoroughly follow a speculative theology (i.e., a non-dualistic, dialectical theology) is the consequent movement of the concept of God into unusual territory. Indeed, it is quite jarring *not* to think of God as a transcendent, positive, external substance responsible for and guaranteeing that all will go well according to the divine plan. Instead, God is the immanent, dynamic movement of a complex positivity that is cut through with negativity. Negativity, then, is the "heart" of (the) God(-World relation) since it is negativity that makes life and identity possible. In other words, there is no hard kernel of substance that exists at the core of Being, be it divine or human.

In the classical sense, then, God *is* dead. Just because one fully endorses a *particular* death of God does not mean that God is entirely dead. God exists but only insofar as the World exists. And to think of this as a simultaneous relationship is difficult to maintain. Nevertheless, this is the truth of speculative Being as Becoming; the ontological state of Being is complex Becoming by way of negativity.

A speculative doctrine of God begs the question, "What does it mean for God to be personal?" True, to be personal means to be able to relate to something. This, however, does not mean that whatever is being related to is ontologically Other. The key within a speculative ontology is to maintain the *differentiated* relationality amidst nondualism. In other words, to be personal is to be related without being reduced to singularities. In this sense, we are the differentiated relations involved in the processes of the life of God. For Hegel, God is that for which there is no externality. And, when one does away with externality, one also does away with internality. Therefore, a speculative reading of Yong's ontological categories of relationality, rationality, and dynamism interprets them not only as being indicative of God but also of the World.

God is only personal insofar as God is related to the world; there is no essential core to God's being that exists on its own. *God, therefore, simultaneously shapes and is shaped by the World.* In this speculative sense, divine personalism is not a substantial entity that acts unilaterally upon the world as Yong claims. Rather, divine personalism only makes rational sense insofar as self-awareness occurs in and through the moments of dynamism via relationality. Every Godly act implies the participation of the World; and every Worldly act implies the participation of God.

By extension, divine personalism is neither panentheistic nor pantheistic. Regarding panentheism, if God does not exist prior to or outside of the World, then God does not create space for the World to inhabit. Regarding pantheism, God and World do not collapse into one another because the identities of both are uniquely complex and connected. In short, God and the World cannot be split into two nor can they be smashed into one. The speculative mode of the dialectic demonstrates an ontology of relationality that no longer holds divine transcendence as something external but instead as that which exists and unfolds in and through the World. This radical break from a dualistic metaphysic into speculative dialectics might be seen as unorthodox or even heretical; nevertheless, it is entirely worth the shock if a nondualistic systematic theology is the goal. Indeed, the revolutionary road is terrifying yet necessary in order for perspectives to be changed. As Žižek states, "a radical act of Good *has* to appear first as 'evil', as disturbing the substantial stability of traditional mores."[10]

Nevertheless, the movement that fills out the process of divine identity is demonstrated by Hegel's "speculative sentence," which was previously discussed; namely, with the Subject as coming *to be* in Predication.[11] In light of the speculative relationship of the Subject-Predicate, the problem to work through with clarity is the immanent versus economic Trinity. The problem is when the immanent Trinity is identified as existing in the Subject position whereas the economic Trinity is identified as existing in the Predicate position, separately. Moreover, the immanent is not affected by the economic. Here, the immanent-economic relationship is non-speculative insofar as the Subject is *not* ontologically connected to Predication thus grounded in a classic substance metaphysic.

This non-relation of the Subject and Predicate (e.g., immanent and economic) contrasts with the speculative relation wherein the Subject moves into the Predicate position, thus transitioning from the abstract to the concrete (Subject➔Subject-Predicate) and then to the individual Subject (Subject-Predicate➔Subject). The individual Subject, mind you, is not the Subject apart from the Predicate but the continuous integration of concrete particularities. In the words of Žižek, the "return move" to the subject occurs when the "*predicate passes into subject*" and the subject is "re-totalized by what was originally its predicate, its subordinated moment."[12] Moreover, the "return move" from the initial position marks the paradigmatic change from a classical definition of substance to a speculative one. As Žižek expounds,

> Yes, in the "negation of negation" the Spirit does "return to itself"; it is absolutely crucial, however, to bear in mind the "performative" dimension of this return: the Spirit changes in its very substance through this return-to-itself—that is, *the Spirit to whom we return, the Spirit that returns to itself, is not the same as the Spirit that was previously lost in alienation.* What occurs in between is a kind of transubstantiation, so that this very return-to-itself marks the point at which the initial substantial Spirit is definitely lost.[13]

And,

> The key moment in the dialectical process involves the "transubstantiation" of its focal point: what was at first just a predicate, a subordinate moment . . . becomes its central moment, retroactively degrading its presuppositions, the elements out of which it emerged, into its subordinate moments, elements of its self-propelling circulation.[14]

Put bluntly, the subject is a process of relation and becoming since there is no subject prior to predication.[15] The type of relation between the positions of subject and predicate is therefore a dynamic one that lets go of the antiquated idea that substance (and/or matter) is isolated and inert.

Because of Yong's strong dialectical leanings in philosophy and movement beyond static formalism in theology, his work is primed for coherent nondualism by piercing into the speculative mode of the trinitarian dialectic.[16]

For example, he claims that "process metaphysics reflects a paradigm shift from the classical ontology of being to an ontology of becoming, and in that respect, provides solid underpinnings for a relational metaphysic."[17] He also affirms C. S. Peirce's epistemological "triadicity [that] avoids the intractable dualisms that have plagued modern thinking on all fronts," thus identifying thought as crossing "the disastrous chasm separating modern construals of mind and matter and of spirit and nature."[18] Yet he holds onto the theological claim that God is, at some point, wholly Other, which is why the goal of moving beyond a classical theory of substance fails to impact the categories of infinite and finite insofar as God qua Spirit *subsists* regardless of the World. However much the theologian critiques dualism, if the God-World relation is not thoroughly desubstantialized, then the entire frame is compromised. While I understand the reasoning behind this preservation of God as (big) Other, to go the dialectical distance, one must accept the fact that this preservation will prevent theology from truly sublating classical dualism.

To extend Yong's theology into a consistent nondualism, I offer a speculative reading of his treatment of the immanent and economic dimensions of the Trinity as this was the main trinitarian problem addressed in the previous chapter. For Yong, all that human beings can know about God has to do with the economic dimension of the Trinity, while the unknown depths of God have to do with the immanent dimension of the Trinity. The immanent Trinity, then, is a non-issue even though it persists as a specter. Nevertheless, he continues to delve deeper into the divine abyss by touching upon the ontological relationship between God and the World via Neville, who wonders about the "indetermination" of God outside of the economic dimension insofar as God becomes God with the World.[19] If so, the immanent dimension turns into a projection of human desire to avoid the instability of uncertainty.

Standing on the precipice of the speculative, Yong retracts with the assertion that "we should not move too quickly from God being indistinguishable from nothing to God as nothing."[20] This is only a problem, though, if there are two separate dimensions of the economic and immanent. Apart from the World, God *is* nothing because there is nothing outside of the World. The speculative reading goes all the way here by positing a singular dimension of immanence. Indeed, God is only God in relation to the World because the World is all there is.

One way of clearly endorsing the speculative mode of dialectics is to radicalize Yong's claim that only the economic dimension of God can be known by replacing it with the economic dimension of God is all there is. The immanent dimension is not simply being cut off and dispensed with; rather, it marks the whole system. Hence, the identities and relationships of Father, Son, and Spirit are all historically determined, and there is no special substance and/or relation that exists on its own, apart from the world.

Whereas Yong only ponders the possibility that God is God only in relation to the World, I commit to such an understanding because it fits rationally and cohesively with a contemporary nondualistic interpretation of the God-World relationship.

In a speculative logic of God, it is impossible to privilege one thing over the other—divine or human—because all things are, at least potentially, in relation. For instance, a person cannot be a person without the experience and presence of other persons, that is, objects are what they are in relation to other objects. In the same way, the Holy Spirit is unable to be privileged over and against the Father and the Son as it can happen in substance logic. Father, Son, and Spirit are reconceptualized as not only dependent on one another for identity but also dependent upon the many identities within the World. This speculative truth is made visible in the incarnation insofar as the finite and infinite are conjoined, which signifies the universality of substance as subject. The melding of the infinite and finite in the particularity of Jesus turns into universality insofar as Jesus is the revelation of God in the World. It is no surprise that it took the combination of God and the World for the picture of Jesus to make sense. It is the *communicatio idiomatum* that sparks the absolute quality of the Becoming of both God and World.

As is typical of Yong, he is both eloquent and vibrant in his elaboration of the role and function of the metaphysical category of spirit. What if the following description of spirit actually describes the Spirit? Namely, "metaphysical commonality," "energetic field," and "dynamic aspect of reality" as describing the ontological aspects of the infinite within the infinite-finite dialectic.

> First, spirit at the metaphysical level points to that which sustains commonality—both human and cosmic. Our common human experience points to our mutually shared and publicly owned world. At the same time, our discrete experiences in and of this world point beyond themselves and is suggestive of a common relational context. Second, spirit points to the energetic or field dimension that sustains the concrete or phenomenological aspects of things in the world. The important qualification here is that "thing" is also a technical metaphysical term and should not be understood as referring only to material objects. Lastly, spirit points to the dynamic aspect of things, the same qualification holding.[21]

To follow these conceptualizations through, the speculative interpretation would be to see the moment when such infinite activity is presented as self-reflexive when caught up in the throes of finite particularization, that is, the infinite becomes self-reflexive only in relation to the finite. This divine conceptualization of what it means to say that God is Spirit, according to Žižek, plays on Schelling's thought on "God's fall . . . into the Openness of time."[22] Of course, a speculative reading does not endorse the literal interpretation of

104   *Chapter 5*

God creating the World because God is indeterminate apart from the World. In this sense, God is not wholly other but wholly complex.

DIALECTICS AND NEGATIVITY

Moving on, there are four problems with Yong's interpretation of Hegel that need to be addressed for the integration of a Hegelian speculative dialectic as interpreted and disseminated by Žižek.[23] First, Hegel's *Geist* is not the Holy Spirit but "the totality of his philosophical system inclusive of its self-determining development."[24] To bolster this interpretation, Cyril O'Regan claims that Hegel's

> Spirit does not denote a particular aspect of the divine, either a particular person of the Trinity as theological orthodoxy would have it or as a specific set of acts, but rather the divine considered in its entirety and exhaustive compass of its acts.[25]

Finally, Žižek puts this broader understanding of *Geist* into perspective by way of the speculative Subject where "a thing is the result of the process (event) of its own becoming."[26] If Yong is aware of this broader understanding of *Geist,* it is not mentioned. This is important because, for Hegel, *Geist* is not God per se but a metaphor that encapsulates the entirety of the God-World network.

Second, Yong validates Hegel's disruption of the dyadic structures of identity with the separation of the infinite from the finite.[27] However, Yong retains the idea that infinite and finite are separate substances that need to be put into communication, not realizing that Hegel is arguing for their ontological unity since God is not a "fixed Subject."[28] Yong misses the implications of the speculative mode of the dialectic in Hegel's reason (*Vernunft*) wherein externality and one-sidedness are sublated.[29]

Third, Hegel does not sacrifice concrete particularity in Absolute Spirit as Yong thinks, which is why Yong prefers Peirce's Secondness over and against Hegel's Speculative.[30] As Yong writes,

> if Kant's critical philosophy promoted no more than a phenomenological metaphysics and Hegel's *Geist* sublated history, Peirce's triadic metaphysics neither succumbed to Kant's skepticism (since reality is now triadically related rather than dyadically divided between phenomenon and noumena) nor lost the sight of real history.[31]

In contrast, one of Žižek's strongest claims is that Hegel is the materialist thinker par excellence because of his nonreductive materialism, that is, the "non-All" quality of materiality within the material-immaterial dialectic. Furthermore, if Hegel's so-called synthesis were to occur and get rid of all negativity and particularity by conflating thesis and antithesis into a totalization, then negativity and difference would disappear, and the system would collapse into undifferentiated sameness.[32]

Fourth, Hegel's dialectic is not the so-called synthesis of thesis versus antithesis that Yong thinks it is.[33] The Hegelian synthesis is not the balancing act of two oppositional poles but the realization that negativity is that which cuts through them both and is involved in their very formation.[34] Synthesis, then, is the "full admission" of the negative that persists in an ontology of Becoming, and the goal is to "enact a parallax shift by which antagonisms are recognized 'as such' and thereby perceived in their 'positive' role."[35] In short, negativity thwarts all attempts to reach a transcendent state of completed perfection.[36] Put bluntly, "forget the story about alienation, loss of the original organic unity, and the return to a 'higher' mediated unity"; rather, the negation of negation is "the shift of perspective which turns failure into true success."[37] As Todd McGowan posits, "if we fail to preserve contradiction, we lose thinking altogether."[38] Hence, according to Hegel, "all things in themselves are contradictory."[39]

Dialectics as ontology embraces perpetual instability and dynamic transformation. The force of the dialectic, made possible by negativity, prevents stasis, collapse, and/or hierarchy, which is why I disagree with Yong's decision to see the Holy Spirit as the engine of the dialectic.[40] As was argued earlier, identifying the Holy Spirit as the engine of the dialectic hinders the sublation of a dualistic God-World model as well as the sacred versus secular, infinite versus finite, transcendent versus immanent, mind versus matter, and spirit versus flesh. Indeed, stacking the dialectic with privilege is problematic in at least two ways: (1) the dialectic cannot be stacked because it is not governable and (2) privilege perpetuates duality. Yong reveals his endorsement of persistent movement with his clarification that a "healthy dialectic" is one that does not stall or "collapse."[41] The solution to the problem of privilege is solved by Yong's claim that the Holy Spirit sustains not just dialectical movement but the dialectic itself. It is the Spirit that breathes life into the dialectical poles of difference for the sake of the whole. In other words, dialectical flow does not stop; it is the breath of God that spurs life on. To posit the Holy Spirit as the curator of the dialectic is to assume that the Holy Spirit is an appendage of an external divine object, thus, in effect, projecting a dialectic that is weighted down by divine positivity. As was pointed out in chapter 4, claiming that the Holy Spirit is the mediator of the dialectic only transposes the fracture of ontological difference from God versus World to Spirit versus World.

In nondualism, however, speculative negativity endorses epistemology as ontology, utilizing the inherent collapse of the dialectic (i.e., contradiction/

106   *Chapter 5*

failure) as the source of energy for constant movement and connection. The solution, then, arrives in the recognition of inherent instability as the persistent source of dynamism.[42] According to Žižek, "Hegel's dialectics is radically groundless, abyssal, a process of the self-relating of the Two which lacks any Third."[43] If a positive third is responsible for maintaining dialectical movement, then the dialectic is no longer fluid, contingent, or open.[44]

In response to Yong's critique of the dialectic becoming nominal and/or collapsible without the presence of the Holy Spirit, this would only occur by the imposition of the theologian. Such dialectical problems only arise when dialectics is seen as an external method, or as non-ontological. Speculative negativity (1) prevents a nominal assessment insofar as dialectics is not just epistemology but also ontology and (2) utilizes the inherent collapse of the dialectic (i.e., contradiction/failure) as energy for movement, deconstruction, and construction. Dialectic is, therefore, shorthand for life insofar as negativity is both destructive and constructive.[45]

Negativity is now expressed as the fissure that runs through God-World identities. Indeed, negativity is a "movement which opens the very place where every positive identity can be situated."[46] In the speculative negation of negation, the Subject realizes that it is directly affected by so-called objective reality, thus turning into a subjectivity wherein both Subject and Object are tied into the same process of Becoming. This transition into speculative subjectivity is the realization that the Subject is involved in the constitution of the Object and vice versa. As Žižek entreats the reader:

> Let us take the "highest" example, that of the crucifixion: the subject first observes the most radical "negation" imaginable, the death of God; then, it becomes aware of how the death of God opens up the space for its own (subjective) freedom.[47]

In thinking about how life emerges from a speculative ontology, it emerges out of a negativity that persists like a wound only to be healed through its acceptance as being part of life.[48] Žižek calls this "ontological dislocation,"[49] that is, life as a painful imbalance to be embraced.[50]

In effect, the origin story goes through a reversal.[51] Life emerges not out of stable positivity but from "the chaotic-psychotic universe of blind drives, their rotary motion, their undifferentiated pulsating."[52] Contrary to the belief that stability precedes disturbance,[53] disturbance is primordial insofar as it participates in the birth of substance as subject and desire.[54] Rather than positing the existence of an external Spirit to preserve dialectical flow, it is the ontological presence of negativity and the resulting flux of Becoming that guarantees such movement.[55]

IMMANENT TRANSCENDENCE

For Yong, the transcendence of God is qualified by objective and unilateral activity. Early on in his work, Yong states that "Classical Christian theology has . . . been correct in emphasizing the divine transcendence and the complete dependence of the world on such a transcendent source."[56] He goes on to say that "theological understanding is a gift of God the Spirit (1. Cor. 2:9-16) whereby the interpreter relies on the gracious (charismatic) activity of the Spirit to reveal and illumine divine truths" that are *otherwise transcendent*."[57] The problem here is the imposition of substantial difference between God and World insofar as God is Other than World, the transcendent source of Thought and Being. The fallout is that human beings remain passive to Spirit, thereby reactionary.[58] The logical conclusion is that the ontological difference between God and World, no matter how big or small, is the irreducible remainder that not only obstructs but also resists a dialectical ontology that, if followed to its end, becomes nondualism.

The interpretation of the transcendence of God is reconceptualized by the speculative dialectic by being placed within the coordinates of ontological immanence. In this sense, transcendence is shorthand for the creative movement of the subject. The transcendence of God, then, is the radical emergence of its becoming in and through the presence of the World; thus, implying the full participation of human beings and nature in the being of God. The uniqueness of human beings and of God is preserved without one collapsing into the other.

As has been consistently argued thus far, classical transcendence, wherein the being of God is ultimately separate from the World, is incompatible with the nondualistic relationality that Yong continues to propagate. For this reason, Yong stops short of reimagining the concept of transcendence altogether so that it fits within his own philosophical paradigm of relation. The specific problem, again, is that Yong adheres to a version of classical transcendence wherein the essential core of God's being is ontologically external to the World.

The problem with these understandings of transcendence is that they conceptually posit the ontological difference between God and the World insofar as the *essential* being of God is other than the (non-)essential being of the World. In other words, God is the transcendent source of Being and Thought and, in turn, the World is dependent. In effect, human beings are (1) passively related to the transcendent Spirit; therefore, (2) human participation is reasonably defined as reactionary performance.[59] The logical conclusion is that the ontological difference between God and the World, no matter how big or small, is *the* irreducible remainder that not only obstructs but actively resists a dialectical ontology that, if followed to its end, would break out of a dualistic

108   *Chapter 5*

frame of transcendence versus immanence. No matter how much one would like, this classical remnant is incompatible with dialectical nondualism. In Žižek's terminology, it is incompatible with a *speculative* transcendence within the immanence frame.

In the speculative frame, transcendence identifies the subjective overcoming of both internal alienation and external limitation without doing away with either. Alienation and limitation are the gaps and walls that give substance to subjectivity. In this sense, the World participates in the self-overcoming of God, thereby giving birth to the finite-infinite subjectivity altogether. God, then, is not a predetermined thing but the radical unfolding of *Geist* in and through the World. The transcendence of God thus implies human participation in the continual birth of finite-infinite dynamics and the inclusion of all things in the Becoming of Spirit.

To be clear, the speculative relation of God and World does not cancel out the possibility of divine personhood. To quote Hegel on this point, "One may define believing in God how one will, but if personality is not there, the definition is inadequate."[60] According to Findlay, Hegel's God "transcends the distinction of persons" insofar as the divine aspect of *Geist* is "most fully manifest in the various *intersubjective* norms which raise conscious experience above what is merely personal and finite."[61] The personhood of God, therefore, sublates the modern understanding and delimitation of what personhood is or can be insofar as it is now defined by *relationality* rather than *individuality*. To be personal, in the speculative sense, is to be relational; and personhood is defined by self-relation vis-à-vis the relationality of the whole, that is, the split person amidst the split whole. Therefore, the subject-object distinction *is* obliterated insofar as the subject is subject in relation to the object and vice versa. Within the speculative dialectic, *divine* personhood is not a *thing* but a *way* of becoming wherein the rigid boundaries that have been put up by classical metaphysics have been seen from a different perspective insofar as they are seen as complex, temporary instantiations.

Žižek rises to the occasion when he claims that the philosophical truth of the Trinity is twofold: (1) oneness requires threeness and (2) actualization requires concrete particularity, that is, "God's manifestation in human history is part of his very essence."[62] In this sense, not only does the personhood of God reveal relational plurality but that divine personhood develops through the incarnation. Žižek imagines God "no longer a monarch who eternally dwells in his absolute transcendence . . . beyond all human history and comprehension"[63] but going "to the end" by

> throw[ing] himself into his own creation, fully engaging himself in it up to dying, so that we humans, are left with no higher Power watching over us, just

with the terrible burden of freedom and responsibility for the fate of divine creation, and thus of God himself.[64]

To think of divine personhood beyond classical conceptualization is no easy feat; it requires the flexibility of thought necessary for moving beyond personhood as static and individual to processual and relational. Entering into a speculative dialectic that is consistent throughout requires concepts being unhindered by dualistic interventions. Yong desires to preserve the "paradoxical tension between the recognition of the Spirit as a divine Thou over and against the I . . . and yet a union between the Spirit and the self that *obliterates* the subject-object distinction."[65] It cannot be both, though. Either (1) the transcendence of God is "Thou over and against the I" or (2) the transcendence of God gets reconceptualized by the "union between the Spirit and the Self that obliterates the subject-object distinction." There are no finer points to consider; the choice is rather simple. Coherent nondualism chooses the latter, allowing conceptual transformation to occur instead of stalling their movement with traditional preservation. In a letter to a friend and pastor, August Tholuck, Hegel proclaims: "I am a Lutheran. And my philosophy has always confirmed me in my Lutheranism."[66] Indeed, the Lutheran theology of the cross bolsters Hegel's integration of the negative in divine nature.[67]

THE FUTURE(S) OF GOD

As was mentioned already, the reason that Yong promotes the classical view of transcendence is to (1) avoid an "anemic eschatology," (2) ensure that God can "experience us in the depth of our existential subjectivities," and (3) prevent "the reverse intuition deriving from ecstatic religious experiences (like that claimed at times by Pentecostals and charismatics) that there is a direct encounter with transcendence (divinity) beyond the split between object and subject."[68] It is important to respond to these three concerns for the sake of properly understanding what a speculative modification of Yong's theology actually is.

First, while the inability of God to unilaterally act upon the world might feel like an "anemic eschatology" insofar as there is no guarantee of a final outcome where perfection is achieved by the final act of God, it is far more consistent and compelling to think of eschatology as ultimately dependent upon the God-World network as a whole and not God alone. This is not a denial of God being able to act, but rather a critique of *how* God acts. More importantly, it is a critique of dualism in the form of divine consummation. Even still, there is no perfect end as there will always need to be the presence of negativity for new life, for better or worse.

Second, divine personalism, no longer understood in the classical way, does not mean that God is, by necessity, unable to experience the existential depth of human beings. In fact, it makes better sense that God would be able to experience humans even more profoundly in dialectical nondualism. Contrary to what Yong believes, any kernel of dualism present within the God-World relationship is a hindrance to God understanding the human experience. This is why the speculative interpretation of the incarnation is so important. As Žižek writes, "the subject, at its very core, also stands for finitude, the cut, the gap of negativity, which is why God only becomes subject through Incarnation: he is not already in himself, prior to Incarnation, a mega-Subject ruling the universe."[69]

In Hegel's Christology, a speculative interpretation of the incarnation, death, and resurrection of Jesus Christ occurs. In the second constitutive moment of the Trinity, that is, self-differentiation, the absolute idea necessarily distinguishes itself from itself through a negating moment. The result of this self-differentiation is the moment of the incarnation, manifesting as the "monstrous compound," the radical relation of the finite and the infinite dimensions within the same Spirit, which is necessary for the self-consciousness of the (God-World) whole.[70] In the words of Hegel, "only the absolute idea determines itself and is certain of itself as absolutely free within itself because of this self-determination."[71] In short, in order for there to be wholeness, the Absolute Idea must go through differentiation to gain self-consciousness and then experience the eternal return-to-itself; all of which are funded by the power of the negative.

Hegel's speculative Christology testifies that "through the infinite anguish of death comes the infinite love of reconciliation."[72] A reconciliation not within the identity of the trinitarian life but also within the speculative God-World life. He locates consciousness as the seat of spirit; in other words, consciousness envelops both faith and knowledge as the place where spirit witnesses to Spirit.[73] Moreover, one's consciousness is not a flight of imagination but a negated (i.e., finite) form of Divine consciousness, "thus both an independent being, an actual being in-and-for-itself, and [b] I as the one who knows of it, are contained within this consciousness of God."[74] Metaphorically speaking, it is "religious knowledge as elevation to God" insofar as both aspects of the God and World are necessary for the becoming of the Absolute Spirit.[75]

Employing Hegel's triadic syllogism of Universal, Particular, Individual, Žižek identifies the incarnation as the Particular—the vanishing mediator responsible for the transition from abstract to concrete. And the Christ event as a whole is made possible not by divine substance but by divine negation.[76] There is no trick being played on the community of believers; Jesus as God is crucified, and the resurrection becomes the symbol of love. God the Father (the Universal) empties/negates into the Particularity of Jesus Christ who faces the crucifixion as negation: "My God, my God, why have you forsaken me?" The resurrection symbolizes, then, the Individual notion of a political theology that quite literally becomes the body of God. Therefore, the Holy Spirit is not a substantial divine being but the identity of "the community of believers."[77] Thus, eternal life as "given to all who believe" is a "purely parallactic" move in perspective, defining eternity as the ultimate commitment to the present rather than a substantial resurrection.[78] The spirit of the community as the Holy Spirit is the "desubstantialized virtual space of the collective of believers."[79] No doubt, a speculative God-World relation that is no longer defined by a classical substance metaphysic is disturbing.

Third, a speculative interpretation of the finite-infinite relationship does consist of "a direct encounter with transcendence (divinity) beyond the split between object and subject" because dualism is no longer. Put differently, the negativity that cleaves all subjects is the same negativity that unites all subjects. A does not directly experience B because A is not entirely separated from B; A is already linked to B. Subjectivity is now defined by pluralism rather than individualism. In short, the *direct* experience of God takes on a whole new meaning: the World is directly wrapped up in the Becoming of God, and both God and World are shaping and being shaped in their dynamic co-emergence.[80]

The point is that the phenomenological surface of being is not an illusion that is hiding a substantial core beyond surface recognition; rather, surface recognition is all there is. Thus, akin to the shift from epistemology into ontology, phenomenology also turns into ontology insofar as there is no predetermined teleological motor that is driving the surface of Being or responsible for the course of history. Rather, the dialectical course of Becoming is contingency, event, and process by way of negativity. In the same way that the Trinity is only economic—that is, no hiddenness/impenetrable substantial core of the Trinity—human beings are only economic, which is why Becoming is prioritized in a speculative dialectical ontology.

In line with the eschatological-trinitarian theologians of the twentieth century, Yong prefers to speak of God as being in the future.[81] In the speculative option for the Trinity as economic, immanence becomes conceptual shorthand for the totality of the God-World relationship, whereas transcendence becomes the openness of all identities within the immanent frame. Transcendence implies plasticity, plurality, and becoming. In short, transcendence represents the ongoing, dynamic future of dialectical immanence.

In this vein, Žižek follows the mystical trajectory of Meister Eckhart's theological understanding. However, the problem that Žižek runs into with Eckhart's trajectory is the theological progression from divine positivity (i.e., the personal nature of God) to divine negativity (i.e., the mystical nature of

112 *Chapter 5*

God). Eckhart moves from the positive being of God to the negative Void of God since it is this Void that provides the setting for the union of God and human beings.[82] For Eckhart, divine positivity exists prior to divine negativity whereas, for Žižek, divine negativity exists prior to divine positivity. Hence, Žižek opts for Hegel's "substance as subject" wherein the "subject does not come first"; Subjectivity "is a predicate-becoming-subject, a passive screen asserting itself as a First Principle, i.e., something posited which retroactively posits its presuppositions."[83] The subject thinks that it has always been there when in reality it has not; the subject emerges out of non-subjectivity. Subjectivity has, does, and will always retain the cut of negativity. Therefore, in contrast to Eckhart's progression from positivity to negativity, Žižek runs with Hegel who moves "not from God to Godhead, but from Godhead to God," that is, not from divine positivity to divine negativity, but from divine negativity to divine positivity.[84]

How, then, should the divine act of creation be understood in light of the nondualistic God-World relationship as well as ontological contingency? With such a loaded question, it is best to begin with the traditional narrative and then move into the philosophical conceptualizations thereof. This method is a Hegelian one wherein theology begins with representations, moves into conceptualizations, and then back to representations. One begins with the traditional narrative of *creatio ex nihilo* wherein God "did not only transform or (re)organize some preexisting stuff, he effectively posited the created universe 'out of nowhere', relying on no preexisting reality."[85] It is this quality of *ex nihilo* that begins to shed light on the *miraculous* nature of the creative act within Christianity that provides the basis for new interpretive territory. As Žižek observes,

> insofar as we consider God and man as two substances, the perfect-infinite-uncreated one and the imperfect-finite-created one, there can be no relation of *identity* between the two, only an external relation (of analogy, of cause and effect . . .); it is only with regard to Godhead, to "*ungod/Unding*" in God, that man can be identical to God.[86]

Infinite substance must be in relation to finite substance from the (theoretical) start; otherwise, dualism will trump nondualism every time. Therefore, it is not that God first creates nothingness out of somethingness and then out of nothingness creation is created; rather, nothingness is at the constitutive center of God's Becoming. This is absolutely imperative if God and World are going to be non-dualistically framed insofar as it is negativity rather than positivity that unites the finite with the infinite. It is the gap within human subjectivity that overlaps with the gap within divine subjectivity that places the two in a properly speculative relation.

The speculative interpretation of *creatio ex nihilo*, however, does not simply adhere to the position that nothingness exists at the center of divine Becoming as if God created nothingness externally thereby not being essentially divine. Rather, the speculative interpretation of *creatio ex nihilo* posits that God *is* this nothingness insofar as creation emerges out of nothing. Obviously, this turn of phrase requires the flexibility of mind to think dialectically since one can never get at the truth directly. God is this nothingness that doesn't turn positive but is seen as positive from a different angle. As Žižek clarifies the flow of pure nothingness to reflexive nothingness, "before determinate differences, there should be . . . a pure difference, a difference in pure intensity which cannot be pinned down to any distinction in qualities or properties."[87] Hence, the becoming of God is not a positive quality or set of properties to be immediately grasped; rather, the becoming of God is only identifiable indirectly insofar as God is that which emerges by way of the self-reflexive negative. As Žižek explains,

> What this means is that there is a Hegelian dialectical reversal to be accomplished here: the initial opposition—"nothingness" as the mode of appearance (to us, finite minds) of the infinite actuality of the creative power of God, i.e., as the "for us" of the unfathomable divine In-Itself—should be turned around, so that God as the supreme Creator, as the highest being, is, on the contrary, the way "nothingness" has to appear to us, finite minds. From this perspective it is, rather, nothingness which stands for the divine In-Itself, and the mirage of God as the Highest Being for God in the mode of his appearance, in his "for-us."[88]

God does not exist at any singular point on the historical timeline that does not include the existence of the World. This is difficult to accept because it challenges traditional understandings of divine creation and culmination, and everything in between. This drastic change of perspective, however, is necessary for a nondualistic God-World relationship to be entirely consistent. One does not need to drop the existence of God altogether; rather, it is primarily the philosophical understanding of the theological narratives that needs sublating. If this conceptual change of perspective is not instantiated, theology is left behind by being defined by classical philosophy and the dualistic relationship of the God-World therein.

NOTES

1. Paul Ricoeur, "Religion, Atheism, and Faith," in *The Conflict of Interpretations: Essays in Hermeneutics*, ed. Don Ihde (Evanston: Northwestern University Press, 1974), 448.

2. This binary of *promotional* versus *reactionary* is similar to what John Caputo and Michael Scanlon have termed "hypertranscendence" and "post-transcendence."

The former describes the doubling down of classical transcendence wherein God is a big Other, whereas the latter describes the emptying of transcendence altogether into immanence. Cf. John Caputo and Michael Scanlon, eds. *Transcendence and Beyond: A Postmodern Inquiry* (Bloomington and Indianapolis: Indiana University Press, 2007), 2–5.

3. Hegel, in his critique of precritical metaphysics, writes that "it is however only in reference to the history of philosophy that this Metaphysic can be said to belong to the past: the thing is always and at all places to be found, as the view which the abstract understanding takes of the object of reason. And it is this point that the real and immediate good lies of a closer examination of its main scope and its *modus operandi*." G. W. F. Hegel, *The Encyclopedia of the Philosophical Sciences: The First Part of the Encyclopedia of the Philosophical Sciences in Outline* (Oxford: Oxford University Press, 1950), §27.

4. Ricoeur, *Freud and Philosophy*, 531.

5. Yong, *The Spirit Poured Out on All Flesh*, 131.

6. Yong, *The Spirit of Creation*, 163.

7. Yong, *The Spirit of Creation*, 163.

8. See Yong, *The Spirit of Creation*, chapters 2, 5, and 6.

9. Taylor, *After God*, 343.

10. Žižek, *Less Than Nothing*, 107.

11. Restated, prior to the event of the Subject-Predicate process, the Subject is just a bundle of contingencies on the move.

12. Žižek, *Less Than Nothing*, 234.

13. Žižek, *Metastases of Enjoyment*, 190. See also Žižek, *The Indivisible Remainder*, 126.

14. Žižek, *Less Than Nothing*, 234.

15. Žižek, *Absolute Recoil*, 29.

16. For example, Yong writes: "Believers encounter the living Christ who is present, understood not in the physicalist or consubstantive terms of Aristotelian and neoscholastic substance philosophy but in the interpersonal and intersubjective terms of contemporary pneumatological theology." Yong, *The Spirit Poured Out on All Flesh*, 163–4.

17. Yong, *Spirit-Word-Community*, 91.

18. Yong, *The Spirit Poured Out on All Flesh*, 288–89.

19. Yong, *Discerning the Spirit(s)*, 106–7.

20. Yong, *Discerning the Spirit(s)*, 107n11.

21. Yong, *Spirit-Word-Community*, 15.

22. Žižek, "The Fear of Four Words," 105n71.

23. See the following summaries on the varieties of misinterpretations that continue to plague contemporary Hegelian interpretations: Adams, *Eclipse of Grace*, "Preface"; McGowan, "The Necessity of an Absolute Misunderstanding," 43–56; Clayton Crockett and Creston Davis, "Risking Hegel: A New Reading for the Twenty-first Century," in *Hegel and the Infinite: Religion, Politics, and Dialectic*, eds. Slavoj Žižek, Clayton Crockett, and Creston Davis (New York: Columbia University Press, 2011), 1–18.

Dialectical Modifications 115

24. Schlitt, *Hegel's Trinitarian Claim*, 2.

25. Cyril O'Regan, *The Heterodox Hegel* (New York: SUNY Press, 1994), 29–30.

26. Žižek, *Absolute Recoil*, 192.

27. Yong, "A Theology of the Third Article?" 218.

28. Hegel, *Phenomenology of Spirit*, §62.

29. Žižek, *Absolute Recoil*, 352.

30. This accusation is confusing given Yong's realization that *Aufhebung* is both the cancellation and preservation of oppositional determinations. See Yong, "A Theology of the Third Article?" 225.

31. Yong, *The Spirit of Creation*, 119. See also Yong, *Spirit-Word-Community*, 117n9.

32. Granted, the accusation that Hegel is, in the end, a rationalizing totalizer is a common misconception by many modern and postmodern thinkers. Pamela Sue Anderson writes, "Ricoeur claims to set Kant's unresolved dialectics of theoretical and practical reason against Hegel's totalizing dialectics of absolute knowledge." Pamela Sue Anderson, *Ricoeur and Kant: Philosophy of the Will* (Atlanta: Scholars Press, 1993), 21. Richard Kearney writes, "This limitation on the pretensions of speculative reason signals for Ricoeur a renunciation of Hegel and all other versions of systematic closure." Richard Kearney, *On Paul Ricoeur: The Owl of Minerva* (Burlington, VT: Ashgate, 2004), 4. Allison Scott-Baumann writes, "Hegel, as the master of dialectical negation, proved to be an invaluable yet ultimately disappointing companion for Ricoeur, because of Hegel's totalizing tendencies, bringing the negative into a grand scheme that removed its power to subvert." Allison Scott-Baumann, *Ricoeur and the Negation of Happiness* (New York: Bloomsbury, 2013), 13. Dan Stiver writes, "Deeply influenced by both philosophers, Ricoeur rejected Hegel's grasping at absolute knowledge, preferring the Kantian limits on knowledge of the thing-in-itself." Dan Stiver, *Ricoeur and Theology* (New York: Bloomsbury, 2012), 10.

33. Yong, *Spirit-Word-Community*, 105. In contrast to synthesis as totalization, J. N. Findlay writes: "Hegel will . . . marvelously include in his final notion of the final state of knowledge the notion of an endless progress that can have no final term. For he conceives that, precisely in seeing the object as an endless problem, we forthwith see it as not being a problem at all." Findlay, "Foreword," xiv.

34. In other words, "the gap is what sets in motion the dialectical movement proper." Žižek, *For They Know Not What They Do*, xxvi.

35. Žižek, *Less Than Nothing*, 225, 819. Elsewhere, J. N. Findlay posits that "Hegel does *not* think that the harmonies of Reason involve any mere rejection of the disharmonies and contradictions of dialectical thought. These disharmonies may be 'overcome' but their overcoming is also their perpetual preservation. For they are overcome only in the sense that they are seen to be necessary conditions of a reasonable result, and so, in a sense, *not* overcome at all. One may, in fact, say, with some exaggeration, that for Hegel the overcoming of contradictions and irrationality consists really in their permanent acceptance, since they are seen to be essential to, and therefore part of, the final rational outcome." Findlay, *Hegel*, 67.

36. Žižek, *The Puppet and the Dwarf*, 140.

116   *Chapter 5*

37. Žižek, *The Parallax View*, 27.

38. McGowan, "The Necessity of an Absolute Misunderstanding," 46.

39. Hegel, *Science of Logic*, 381.

40. See Yong, *Spirit-Word-Community*, 14.

41. "Previous theological methodologies either fail to sustain the dialectical movement or collapse the dialectic altogether because they lack a pneumatological 'engine'. I will endeavor to show that a vital pneumatology is indispensable for a truly healthy dialectic in that it drives the to-and-fro movement necessary to sustain both poles." Yong, *Spirit-Word-Community*, 14.

42. For a discussion on the positivity of contradiction vis-à-vis historical pentecostalism, see Hollenweger, *Pentecostalism*, 195.

43. Žižek, *Less Than Nothing*, 303.

44. See Žižek, *Organs without Bodies*, 65.

45. For a discussion on the positivity of contradiction vis-à-vis historical pentecostalism(s), see Hollenweger, *Pentecostalism*, 195.

46. Žižek, *The Sublime Object of Ideology*, 199–200.

47. Žižek, *Less Than Nothing*, 299.

48. Žižek, *The Sublime Object of Ideology*, 199.

49. Žižek, *Less Than Nothing*, 376. See also Carew, *Ontological Catastrophe*, 240.

50. Žižek, *The Sublime Object of Ideology*, 199.

51. Žižek, *Less Than Nothing*, 475.

52. Žižek, *The Indivisible Remainder*, 13. This is repeated in Žižek, *The Abyss of Freedom*, 14–15.

53. "This, precisely, is what a properly dialectical approach rejects: before transgression there is just a neutral state of things, neither good nor bad (neither property nor theft, neither law nor crime); the balance of this state of things is then violated, and the positive norm (Law, property) arises as a secondary move, an attempt to counteract and contain the transgression." Žižek, "The Fear of Four Words," 71.

54. Žižek is following Lacan on desire, namely, the claim that desire is a projection, that is, *objet petit a*, or object-cause of desire, that will never be reached, thus drawing subjectivity forward not by a positive external impetus but by the internal gap of desire.

55. See Žižek, "The Fear of Four Words," 71–2.

56. Yong, *Discerning the Spirit(s)*, 106.

57. Yong, *Spirit-Word-Community*, 222 (emphasis added).

58. See Amos Yong, *Renewing Christian Theology: Systematics for a Global Christianity* (Waco: Baylor University Press, 2014), 159.

59. See Amos Yong, *Renewing Christian Theology*, 159.

60. Quoted by Dale Schlitt in Schlitt, *Hegel's Trinitarian Claim*, 3.

61. Findlay, *Hegel*, 42–3.

62. Žižek, "The Fear of Four Words," 32.

63. Žižek, "The Fear of Four Words," 32.

64. Žižek, "The Fear of Four Words," 25.

65. Yong, *Discerning the Spirit(s)*, 224 (emphasis added).

66. G. W. F. Hegel, *Hegel: The Letters*, trans. Clark Butler and Christine Seiler (Bloomington: Indiana University Press, 1984), 520.

67. Hegel, *Lectures on the Philosophy of Religion*, 468.

68. Yong, *Discerning the Spirit(s)*, 93n38.

69. Žižek, *Less Than Nothing*, 286. See also, Žižek, *The Puppet and the Dwarf*, 13.

70. Hegel, *Lectures on the Philosophy of Religion*, 457–8. See Hodgson, *Hegel & Christianity*, 90.

71. Hegel, *Lectures on the Philosophy of Religion*, 434.

72. Hodgson, *Hegel & Christianity*, 276.

73. Hegel, *Lectures on the Philosophy of Religion*, 148.

74. Hegel, *Lectures on the Philosophy of Religion*, 135.

75. Hegel, *Lectures on the Philosophy of Religion*, 164.

76. Kotsko, *Žižek and Theology*, 130.

77. Žižek, "Dialectical Clarity Versus the Misty Conceit of Paradox," 292.

78. Žižek, "Dialectical Clarity Versus the Misty Conceit of Paradox," 292.

79. Žižek, "Dialectical Clarity Versus the Misty Conceit of Paradox," 295.

80. See Žižek, *The Puppet and the Dwarf*, 138.

81. Yong, *Discerning the Spirit(s)*, 93n38.

82. Žižek, "The Fear of Four Words," 41.

83. Žižek, *Absolute Recoil*, 29. See also Žižek, *The Most Sublime Hysteric*, 22.

84. Žižek, *Absolute Recoil*, 41.

85. Žižek, "The Fear of Four Words," 42.

86. Žižek, "The Fear of Four Words," 34.

87. Žižek, "The Fear of Four Words," 43.

88. Žižek, "The Fear of Four Words," 43.

Chapter 6

God the Negative

FROM DUALISM TO NONDUALISM

The Sacred Negative

Yong claims that his theological goal has always been to "carve a via media between an inflexible conservativism and an unbridled progressivism."[1] Well aware that conservatives think him too far left and progressives think him too far right, he nevertheless perseveres. My own theological goal is similar in that I seek to cut through the forced choice of God exists or God does not exist. Such a question is far too limiting for a speculative dialectic that presents itself in nondualistic Becoming. Seeking paradigmatic change, I follow Yong's lead into boundary-breaking ideas that no doubt strike many as unorthodox but catalytic nonetheless.

> A foundational pneumatology . . . presupposes the rethinking not only of theology proper but also of cosmology. It aspires to correlate the idea of God with that of the world: God should be the kind of reality that is able both to be present and to act, and the world should be the kind of thing that is able to be the locus of divine presence and activity.[2]

To achieve systemic coherence between philosophy and theology wherein transcendence is immanent, God presents as the negative force that becomes reflexive amidst the relational processes of the Whole. God, then, is no longer a self-enclosed, positive substance because classical metaphysics dissolve in the face of contemporary scientific revisions. My claim is that God is a reflexive disruption that becomes personal in and through the movement and processes of the Whole, and that the identity of God is primarily movement instead of stasis.

120   *Chapter 6*

So, why return to Yong if he does not fully enter the speculative dialectic? Because he provides the theologian with the theological and philosophical paths that point toward speculative becoming.[3] He maps the terrain for others who are also interested in critical versions of pentecostal theology. For instance, he speaks from a pentecostal perspective unafraid of breaking tradition. He promotes interreligious dialogue without the discrete categorizations of exclusivism, inclusivism, or pluralism.[4] Instead, he opens avenues of possible connections with other religions without collapsing the discussion into sameness or difference by emphasizing the fecundity of Spirit.

He also presents a political pneumatology that reconfigures soteriology by claiming that salvation is not "abstract" or hypothetical but rather "the concrete experiences of embodied, social, political, economic, and spiritual beings as the Holy Spirit is poured out on them."[5] While I take issue with the unqualified use of "poured out," I agree with him insofar as an apathetic disposition toward the world made possible by a dispensational eschatology is no longer tenable. Justification is not the mere act of being "made right with God" in the forensic sense; rather, it is primarily the unmasking of evil structures that oppose human dignity and well-being. The Gospel is only "good news" if it moves from edification to revolution in "making concrete God's redemptive activity in all spheres and aspects of life"[6] without resorting to "theological imperialism."[7] Yong's point is that the Spirit is made real by way of righteous relationality and that public pneumatology will inevitably create a new type of "experiential and incarnational logic" that seeks to make sense of the Christian life in new terms.[8]

Unstuck from rigid dichotomies, Yong's theology can follow the "complex determinations of being" throughout the entire system.[9] God is thus an integral dimension of the lifeworld, albeit emerging from the material-immaterial dialectic sustained by negativity. Put differently, God discovers its own subjectivity amidst the collective, and negativity is that which becomes the voice of God amidst the depths of mystery. Altogether, Yong's theology provides a significant thrust out of the monotonous experience of pentecostal dictates. Piercing through the cliché of pious theological language, he peels away the rotting flesh of dying propositions to reveal the textures of complexity and the possibility of renewal. He does this by critiquing dualistic frameworks and pointing out the conceptual relationality of the terms involved in theological ideation. My favorite example being his revision of spiritual gifts as immanent instead of transcendent.[10]

And yet, Yong's critique of the "supernaturalistic inbreaking of the Spirit" needs a stronger bite if the Spirit is to be seen as immanently accessible. And if the Spirit is essentially relational, as Yong claims it to be, then, based upon the premise that negativity is involved in identity formation, it follows that the identity of Spirit is also cut open, resulting in the destruction of divinity as an external, impassive force. Commitment to an ontology of relational becoming suggests the wager be placed upon human participation in the creative becoming of God. Hence, the nondualistic Spirit emerges amidst ontological complexity sustained by negation since it is that which makes movement/change/life possible. Thus, God is no longer an impassive super-agent that creates and sustains the world; rather, God is that which emerges in and through the World.

While this is a good place to start, I travel beyond Yong by identifying negativity as that which makes the God-World network possible. In the speculative mode of dialectics, human participation is actively involved in the becoming of God without assuming, positing, or defaulting to ancient dualism. Indeed, by following speculative logic, theology can sublate dualism and enter the bright horizon of dialectical mysticism. In the same way that Yong describes human identity as complex, so it goes with God.

Materiality and immateriality are not sequestered components that can be put in right relationship because the material and the immaterial are not independent from one another; As was mentioned earlier, Žižek claims that oppositional identities are not brought into contact by way of a transcendent third; rather, one passes into the identity of the other by way of negativity. "The point," according to Žižek, "is that Being in itself, when we try to grasp it 'as it is', in its pure abstraction and indeterminacy, without further specification, reveals itself to be Nothingness."[11] God, therefore, discovers its own substance—that is, discovers its own subjectivity—through reflexive negativity and the actors therein. All of this is a stone's throw away from Yong's ontology of complexity,[12] dynamism,[13] and emergence.[14]

Dialectical Materialism

Žižek's version of dialectical materialism narrates the co-determinate relationality of the material and the immaterial in Becoming; that is, insofar as Becoming remains incomplete and exposes subjects as clusters of negativity, contingency, and event.[15] The goal of "dialectical analysis," then, is "to unearth the contingency of . . . necessity itself" and reveal entities as decentered phenomena that make meaning through reflection and repetition.[16] In this sense, events are "infinite" in that "there is no external limit,"[17] and to be immanent is to be circumscribed by the non-All and its unlimited expanse.

In my version of theology vis-à-vis dialectical materialism, God is the coalescent transubstantiation of human beings into the *virtual reality* of the non-Whole, that is, the saturation of relationality. Since God is not a predetermined thing that subsists on its own apart from the World, it is a subject that gains its substance through the ongoing pulse of the World. In immanence, then, truth is not judged by an e(x)ternal essence of Truth but by human pragmatism wherein the approach toward truth is "the truth itself."[18] All events that occur within immanent becoming imply the creative participation of human beings in the creation of Truth(s). Simply put, if there is no neutral ground by which to judge Truth, then Subjects participate in Truth itself. The standards of truth, then, emerge when "a statement is compared with itself, with its own process of enunciation."[19]

No longer are the sciences driven by the belief that the laws of nature are predictable and that matter is made up of solid objects that bump into one another from a distance.[20] Einstein disproved the former with his theory of relativity, insofar as space and time change depending on speed and velocity, and quantum physics disproved the latter with the inconsistency of matter.[21] The theological lesson of quantum physics, then, is rightly understood by Žižek as supporting the Hegelian integration of absolute negativity within a dialectical ontology of the non-All.[22] The speculative is not simply an ideological truth but one that is supported by contemporary scientific inquiry.

The Speculative God

God is not a wholly Other but the reflexivity that finds its own substance (i.e., subjectivity) through human intersubjectivity; God the Spirit is the subjective and self-conscious aspect of the Whole as non-All. God is becoming. There is, then, a *more than* quality of God amidst the speculative dialectic insofar as God exists amidst the human collective, a virtual reality that is *based upon* the concrete participation of human beings yet *more than* insofar as this virtual reality is actively connected to thoughts and actions. In the same way that the World shapes the becoming of God, so the becoming of God shapes the World. Once again, Yong walks up to the edge of the speculative without crossing over: "not only does the materiality of human embodiment participate in the being of God, so also does the materiality of human cultural achievement reflect the creativity of God."[23] To go all the way with this, God is the symbol of the paradoxical self-reflexive negativity that is neither here nor there but everywhere.

Beyond the opposition of naturalism (i.e., religion as valuation) and supernaturalism (i.e., God as wholly Other), God is neither nothing nor something but less than nothing.[24] God is the "swerve" in the Void that destabilizes rigid reflections that squelch new life.[25] God is not a positive entity that emerges out of the negative Void; rather, God is the negative that maintains the Void, that is, the disruptive movement within negativity that makes reflexivity possible. Perhaps the indeterminate God prior to its simultaneous emergence with the World is disturbance, the negative tremor that breaks forth into mutuality.

God the Negative 123

Whatever the case, thought must allow divine negativity to take its course to sublate the classical versions of metaphysics, ontology, and epistemology and break free from dualistic constraint and move into the relational capacity of nothing. This is what Hegel is arguing for with his profound theme of "tarrying with the negative." If theology is unable to "tarry with the negative," the dialectical process is cut short, thereby reinforcing a dualistic frame of God versus World. To run with negativity is to experience the liberating loss of stasis, to realize that all truths are conditional upon a destruction that clears the way forward.

THE SPECULATIVE DIALECTIC AND PENTECOSTALISM

As one who comes from the classical pentecostal denomination, The Assemblies of God, it is important to not only modify the theology of Amos Yong but also the theology of my foundational community. I chose to begin with the sociopolitical dimension of classical pentecostalism as the nascent harbinger of negativity, that is, the inherent potential of negativity found in pentecostal practice.[26] From there, I followed the conceptual movement of negativity from practice to theory. For example, from the distinctives of early pentecostal practice—for example, racial, social, and gender equality—to the theory of the God-World network.[27] Yong connects this combination of pentecostal praxis and theory in the following way:

> The witness that Spirit Baptism enables is a life and message whose values run counter to the dominant conventions and structures of this world. Perhaps contemporary Christian life ought to be more marginal or exilic than mainstream, as it currently is in various parts of the world.[28]

While negativity is not explicitly identified by practitioners as being functional, it is no less present. Therefore, the possibility of pentecostalism and the speculative dialectic coexisting is now seen as at least arguable.

In early pentecostalism, the social and political practices reveal the presence of negativity and the power of the Spirit, especially in perhaps the most significant pentecostal distinctive of Spirit Baptism. Therein, "values run counter to the dominant conventions and structures of this world," thereby funding a "more marginal or exilic" identity.[29] While negativity is not typically identified by Pentecostals as active in everyday practices, it is no less present. Thus, my argument is the following: (1) Spirit Baptism is an embodiment of God, (2) the sociopolitical practices of Spirit Baptism involve negation, (3) though unnoticed, negativity is present in early pentecostal practices,

124   *Chapter 6*

(4) negativity is best understood through speculative dialectics, and (5) Spirit Baptism is grounded in nondualism. Hence, a critical extension of early pentecostal practices leads to the nondualistic interpretation of the God-World relation. By identifying the role of negativity therein, the coordinates of a speculative dialectic reveal themselves as a latent configuration of the pentecostal movement at least insofar as Spirit Baptism is a key distinctive. As pentecostal scholar Cheryl Bridges Johns makes clear,

> Pentecostals represent many denominations and a variety of theological beliefs. Among the movement's adherents one can find trinitarians and non-trinitarians, those who practice adult baptism only and those who utilize infant and adult baptism. Not all Pentecostals speak in tongues, but none would forbid the practice. There are Catholic Pentecostals, Anglican Pentecostals and a host of separate Pentecostal denominations. There exists no worldwide Pentecostal organization which serves to unify all its adherents. Clearly it is difficult to identify, theologically or sociologically, Pentecostalism. What has generally unified these divergent groups is a belief in the experience known as the baptism of the Holy Spirit following conversion. Many Pentecostals believe that the initial evidence of having received the Pentecostal baptism is that a person will speak, under the Spirit's influence, in unknown tongues. This experience is seen as the bestowing of power for service and the ability to live a holy life. It becomes a "transforming moment" in a believer's life.[30]

In this sense, it is an honest possibility to endorse speculative dialectics and remain distinctively pentecostal.

To be clear, I am not claiming that all early pentecostalism was consciously subversive in a sociopolitical way. Nor am I claiming that all early pentecostalism identified with Spirit Baptism. I am simply arguing that the *coordinates* for a speculative dialectical theology are present within early pentecostalism thus plausible that early pentecostal theology could have developed into a nondualistic speculative ontology of the God-World network.

Frank Bartleman the Social Critic

The origin of a subversive pentecostal theology includes Frank Bartleman's voice, one of the key figures of the Azusa Street Revival who took part in documenting, leading, and critiquing.[31] He is the first pentecostal who published critiques of racism, classism, nationalism, militarism, and capitalism.[32] In what was labeled an "entirely too radical" tract, Bartleman admonishes the pentecostal movement for falling away from "'seven years' of plenty" to "seven years of famine" with the gifts of the Spirit that were once used to build a church upon the suffering love of Christ had become twisted into religious self-conceit, "spiritual indulgence," warmongering, and greed.[33] He thought the movement had lost its "pilgrim identity" by turning in worship toward "the money god."[34] He goes so far as to say that the pentecostal movement had become a "Christless Pentecost."[35]

True to pentecostal identity, Bartleman grounds the nature of the church in the book of Acts, claiming that the socioeconomic equality therein is the Christological principle for how the church should embody and practice political love. In his own words, "what is Christianity good for if it is not practical? . . . We need the 'all things in common' experience of Acts 2 and 4."[36] This political praxis empowered by the Spirit is what instantiates Bartleman's prophetic rebuke of the capitalist system. It is no surprise, then, that while accusing communism of atheism, he welcomes it as a "scourge" sent by God to purify and reignite a remnant of true believers within the pentecostal ranks.[37] Throughout his life, he smashed his pen against the hellish insertion of capitalist values into the pentecostal movement:

> Capitalist Church System must go down, for it is not built on the Word of God. It is a travesty on the Gospel. . . . Poor backslidden, apostate church! . . . It would be a good thing for the kingdom of God if all false shepherds, hireling ministers of the capitalistic church systems, could lose their jobs. And they will . . . Judgment is coming our way.[38]

What became of Bartleman's critiques of a movement that was birthed in a burned-out building? What happened to a movement that "[grew] up almost entirely in the soil of the modern urban slum" and sought to provide an alternative way of being in the early twentieth century?[39]

I offer four reasons: First, it had to do with the loss of an anti-capitalist "prophetic strain" in the transition from first- to second-generation Pentecostals.[40] Second, the ascension in class status between the early to mid-twentieth century culminated in pentecostal organizations joining the National Association of Evangelicals in 1947 and imbibing the voice and force of the religious conservative right.[41] Third, pentecostal publishers and leaders censored early radical ideas that cut against pentecostal institutions and conservative party lines. As Walter Hollenweger has made clear,

> the ferocious mutilation of early Pentecostal writings by Pentecostal publishers will perhaps open the eyes of Pentecostals to what happens to texts . . . when they are passed down in a changing social context and when their message becomes uncomfortable.[42]

Fourth, the movement away from a Wesleyan-Holiness postmillennial eschatology with sanctification that involves sociopolitical and economic dimensions toward a premillennial eschatology with sanctification tied up in preaching and saving souls in preparation for the imminent return of

126   *Chapter 6*

Christ.[43] In short, what started out as a nondualistic embodiment of God with evidence of sociopolitical change in its wake had become a watered-down, dualistic ideology more concerned with the afterlife than the here and now. Ideologically, then, pentecostalism turned into a cosmic dualism suited with total dependence upon the sovereignty of God that led to the claim that direct political engagement was ultimately a waste of time.

Embodiment and Nondualism

James K. A. Smith identifies "five key aspects" of the "Pentecostal social imaginary": (1) "radical openness to God," (2) "enchanted theology of creation and culture," (3) "non-dualistic affirmation of embodiment and materiality," (4) "affective, narrative epistemology," and (5) "eschatological orientation to mission and justice."[44] For me, the most important being the "non-dualistic affirmation of embodiment and materiality" because of its viability as a pathway toward explicit pentecostal nondualism. Yong calls this focus on the embodied experience of the Spirit a "pentecostal sacramentality" in that the Spirit is "being made present and active through the materiality of personal embodiment and congregational life."[45]

Even though the early pentecostal experience of the Spirit is nondualistic insofar as the Spirit is embodied and transformative, the theoretical understanding of such experiences, unfortunately, turned dualistic. As Frank Bartleman writes: "[The Spirit] must be experienced to be understood. It cannot be explained. . . . Only simple faith and abandonment can receive it. Human reason can find all kinds of flaws and apparent foolishness in it."[46] Meaning, God is found and felt in radical spiritual experiences wherein the Spirit is present in their midst, actively creating change in the realm of embodied existence. However, if one has a desire to reflect and systematize on this embodied experience, according to Bartleman, it is impossible due to the finitude of human reason vis-à-vis the inexplicable and unlimited power of the Spirit. The body is accepted as the location of divine experience but rejected as incapable of understanding.

Moreover, according to Bartleman, the body must be destroyed in order to live in the fullness of the Spirit. Bartleman claims that the experience and revelation of the Spirit are only possible at the "place of utter abandonment of will" in the sense of an "absolute consciousness of helplessness" wherein bodies have been "purified from natural self-activity."[47] Simply put, human bodies are the loci of divine experience yet obstacles to be overcome.[48] Simply put, human bodies are welcomed as the loci of divine experience yet rejected as obstacles to be overcome. While I appreciate the sentiment of humility, the body cannot be accepted and rejected at the same time.

A speculative pentecostal theology that embraces the nondualistic frame of the God-World relationship must logically claim that human bodies are to be fully welcomed in all aspects, experiential and rational, insofar as they participate in the ontological becoming of God. The irony of this early pentecostal anti-intellectual reaction against theoretical reflection, of course, is the fact that all beliefs are theoretically based; the reality, though, is that some theories are better than others. And, in this case, nondualism is a better theory than dualism. The still popular pentecostal belief that God is ontologically other than the World—akin to the dualism of spirit and matter[49]—thus beyond human knowing is a product of the enduring Platonic dualism of the finite versus the infinite. As Patrice Haynes makes clear,

> from Plato onwards, the western imaginary has typically figured immanence pejoratively in terms of the limits of matter, the body, sensibility, being, worldliness, etc. This devaluation of material immanence is thoroughly consolidated, according to Nietzschean lines of critique, by the theistic notion of *divine transcendence* used to express God's radical otherness from the world. The transcendent God of theism, so the argument runs, invites a "rhetoric of ascent," which promotes the aspiration to disengage from material finitude, deemed lowly and base, in order to reach up towards spiritual union with the divine, deemed eminent and superior.[50]

Because pentecostal theories went unchecked for so long, the pentecostal meaning-making process became fraught with logical contradictions that plagued the cohesiveness between experience, practice, and theory. For instance, Walter Hollenweger claims that Pentecostals "are strong on experience of the Spirit, on pneuma*praxis*, but they are weak on the interpretation of these experiences."[51] And, by "weak," Hollenweger means the uncritical acceptance of predetermined theological theories that are outdated and contradictory. Hollenweger notes that Pentecostals privilege the Spirit in experience yet subordinate the Spirit under Jesus, thus turning the Spirit's authenticity into a type of "Calvinistic pneumatology" wherein "the Spirit is allowed no dignity in his (or her) own."[52]

According to Smith, the problem of bodily rejection can be resolved by highlighting bodily acceptance in pentecostal healing. As Smith writes,

> implicit in this affirmation of bodily healing is a broader affirmation, namely, a sense that the full gospel values the whole person. In other words, inchoately embedded in this central affirmation that God cares about our bodies is a radical affirmation of the goodness of creation that translates (or *should* translate) into a radical affirmation of the goodness of bodies and materiality as such.[53]

Therefore, the pentecostal appraisal of the body in theo*praxis* is the place from which to carry forward an authentic critical approach to the enduring misinterpretation that the body is something to be rejected; moreover, it is the

128   *Chapter 6*

place to be extended into the speculative understanding of the finite-infinite relationship insofar as God is self-reflexive negativity that binds together a nondualistic experience, practice, and theory of the God-World network.

Perhaps God is the Spirit of dialectical Negativity, the symbol of simultaneous clutching and releasing that eventually softens hardened structures into pliable materials for living.

Spirit Baptism and Negativity

How, then, is negativity identified as present in the theory of Spirit Baptism and human embodiment? If God is the swerve in the Void, the embodiment of God is the embodiment of the Negative. In other words, if God is (speculative) Negativity and the human body is the location of Spirit Baptism, then Negativity runs through God and the World. A speculative interpretation of Spirit Baptism thus turns into a finite-infinite dialectic.

The problem to be addressed, then, is the logical contradiction that exists between (1) the early nondualistic *practice* of classical pentecostalism, that is, the human being's embodiment of the Spirit with evidence of sociopolitical change and (2) the growing dualistic *theory* of classical pentecostalism insofar as God is Other than the World. What needs to happen in order to fix this incoherence is a revised focus on the presence of negativity within pentecostalism. What emerges is a nondualistic God-World relationship that manifests in sociopolitical subversiveness.

The good news is that pentecostal theology is in the midst of revitalization with "[t]he supposed dualism between the material and non-material realms" being "called into question by the ongoing pentecostal-charismatic dialogue."[54] Pentecostal theologies that are intellectually honest do not blindly adhere to authoritarian dictates or institutional reifications; rather, consideration is directed toward themes of liberation and authenticity once again.[55] Such an emerging phase of critical revitalization is a complex endeavor insofar as it calls for the participation of many voices from many backgrounds and the revitalization of ontological connection without reduction. Nevertheless, it is a revitalization that is necessary for philosophical and theological coherence.

As a caveat regarding the many voices that will emerge in this revitalization process, the democratic call for pentecostal participation in theological understanding does not mean that all voices are equally valid and should be accepted without critique. Not all contributions are committed to avoiding logical incoherence. Amidst the various pentecostal contributions, there must be a critical construction of a theological ontology that argues for a nondualistic interpretation of the God-World relationship while promoting pentecostal experience and practice. Otherwise, one's understanding of Self vis-à-vis

God becomes skewed by uninterrogated and/or unreasonable claims. Reason, therefore, must be the ultimate standard of truth rather than an emotional appeal to authority. Therefore, the present call for global pentecostal participation toward inclusive reform must retain the discerning act of rejection for the sake of nondualistic coherence.

Alain Badiou highlights the dialectical relation of inclusion and rejection in his take on the movement from the philosophical to the political. Badiou writes, "Anyone can be a philosopher, or the interlocutor of a philosopher. But it is not true that any opinion is worth as much as any other opinion."[56] Here, Badiou is critiquing the pitfall of postmodernity, which is the slippage into vulgar pluralism. All too often, postmodernity neglects the much-needed power of singularity, thus undermines its ability to interrupt systemic evils due to weakness.[57] Rather than falling victim to the endless roundabout of commentary upon commentary, theology must argue for truth. Namely, the truth of a nondualistic ontology of the God-World relationship and its implicit existence in pentecostalism.

THE SPECULATIVE DIALECTIC AND YONG'S FOUNDATIONAL PNEUMATOLOGY

Amos Yong provides the content for a speculative interpretation of negativity in pentecostal experience, practice, and theory. The presence of negativity within Yong's theology is not only found in the speculative interpretation of his trialectics but also in his "foundational pneumatology" wherein thought moves beneath the theory of Spirit Baptism and into the philosophical claims regarding (1) God as the driving Negativity of the dialectic and (2) God's functional role in and through the World. What emerges is a "foundational pneumatology" of a God-World network curated by God the Negative.

Like Peirce's "contrite fallibilism" and Žižek's non-All, Yong defines "foundational" as "provisional, relative to the questions posed by the community of inquirers, and subject to the ongoing process of conversation and discovery."[58] Yong adds the concept of "shifting foundations" wherein specific concepts and methods used to make sense of theological claims are recognized as constantly changing, depending upon critical and contextual interpretations.[59] The movements consist of the "dialectic of Scripture and experience, of thought and praxis, of theology and doxology, of reason and narrative, of object and subject, of a priori rationality and a posteriori empiricism, of the self and community."[60] The World has access to divine truths because of its direct connection to God and the inherent ability to think through the complexity of content in theological claims without reduction. Because of the ontological quality of negativity in the God-World

130 *Chapter 6*

relationship, divine truths are ontologically incomplete yet epistemologically accessible, that is, (1) relational, rational, and dynamic, (2) immanent, (3) incomplete, and (4) always in motion. God and World are no longer understood as self-contained identities but symbols of the types of relations that exist amidst the incomplete Whole. God the Spirit, that is, God the Negative, is no longer at a distance but that which runs through it all.

By identifying the role and function of the negative within the early pentecostal distinctives of sociopolitical subversiveness and Spirit Baptism, as well as Amos Yong's foundational pneumatology, movement into nondualism has begun. As the motor of the dialectic, negativity, that is, that which separates and unites, undergirds the movement of everything. What dialectical materialism calls for is thought beyond an outdated ontology that has been unable to transition into the critical realm of non-substance. Instead of defaulting to a narrative epistemology, dialectical materialism confronts metaphysics head-on by utilizing the means therein for realizing a pentecostal theology capable of linking theological, philosophical, social, and political movements.

NOTES

1. Amos Yong, *Spirit of Love: A Trinitarian Theology of Grace* (Waco: Baylor University Press, 2012), vii.

2. Yong, *Discerning the Spirit(s)*, 99.

3. I am referring to Yong's theology being mapped onto his critical philosophy.

4. See Yong, *Discerning the Spirit(s)* and *Beyond the Impasse* on how to transcend the soteriological typologies of either inclusivist, exclusivist, or pluralist. In particular, Yong, *Discerning the Spirits*, 55ff.; Yong, *Beyond the Impasse*, chapters one and three; Yong, *Hospitality and the Other*, chapters 3 and 5.

5. Yong, *The Spirit Poured Out on All Flesh*, 120.

6. Yong, *The Spirit Poured Out on All Flesh*, 165.

7. Yong, *Discerning the Spirit(s)*, 58, 144–5.

8. Yong, *The Spirit Poured Out on All Flesh*, 136.

9. Yong, *Beyond the Impasse*, 134.

10. Yong, *Discerning the Spirit(s)*, 175 (emphasis added).

11. Žižek, *The Sublime Object of Ideology*, 194.

12. Yong advocates for the "recognition of the multidimensional character of human life, one that acknowledges the ontological complexity that constitutes the interface of the spiritual and the material domains of this world." Yong, *Spirit of Creation*, 35.

13. Yong, *Spirit-Word-Community*, 15.

14. Yong, *Spirit-Word-Community*, 116.

15. While Žižek consistently sides with Badiou on how to define and understand Event, here he offers commentary on the three thinkers of the Event: Heidegger, Deleuze, and Badiou in Žižek, *The Parallax View*, 165–6.

God the Negative 131

16. Žižek, *Less Than Nothing*, 575. See also Žižek, *Metastases of Enjoyment*, 135n18.

17. Žižek, *Less Than Nothing*, 76–7.

18. Žižek, *The Sublime Object of Ideology*, 68. See also Žižek, *The Sublime Object of Ideology*, 222; Žižek, *For They Know Not What They Do*, 99–100; Žižek, *Organs Without Bodies*, 58; Žižek, *The Parallax View*, 17; Žižek, *Less Than Nothing*, 503–4, 907; Žižek, "The Descent of Transcendence into Immanence or, Deleuze as a Hegelian," 244–5.

19. Žižek, *Less Than Nothing*, 77. He goes on to discuss the role of sophistry in the transition from "mythos" to "logos." Žižek, *Less Than Nothing*, 77. See also, Žižek, *The Parallax View*, 126–7.

20. See Brian Greene, *The Elegant Universe: Superstrings, Hidden Dimensions, and the Quest for the Ultimate Theory* (New York: Vintage Books, 1999), 23ff.

21. Greene, *The Elegant Universe*, 8–9.

22. See footnote 20 and the relationship between quantum physics and evental language.

23. Yong, *In the Days of Caesar*, 236.

24. Žižek, *Less Than Nothing*, 304.

25. Tony Lack, "Review Essay: Slavoj Žižek: Absolute Trouble or Recoil in Paradise?" *Logos* 15:2–3 (Summer 2016), http://logosjournal.com/2015/lack-Žižek-review/.

26. Pentecostalism, in this section, is primarily being defined as early American pentecostalism, which came out of the Azusa Street revival.

27. An example of the early pentecostal distinctive of social equality, Yong comments that "For [William] Seymour, of central significance was not the charismatic phenomenology of the revival but the fact that in the outpouring of the Spirit at Azusa Street, 'the "color line" was washed away in the blood'." Yong, *The Spirit Poured Out on All Flesh*, 72. In the face of rampant racism, classical pentecostalism broke down this barrier insofar as people from all backgrounds worshipped alongside one another in unity and love. In a more radical way, Yong discusses the "resources that black pentecostals ritualized in their Christian worship in order to empower themselves against the challenges posed by racism, sexism, and classism." And, that "black pentecostal worship experience has always included not only the aesthetic dimension but also the ethical: the Spirit's descent, resulting in dancing, clapping, shouting, chanting, the testimony, the sermon, the applause, glossolalia, and even ecstatic possession, works alongside the spirituals, blues, jazz, rhythm, rap, gospel music, and instrumentalizations to empower black communities from week to week in the acts of resistance, rebellion, and reform demanded in their day-to-day existence . . . a spirituality of resistance." Yong, *The Spirit Poured Out on All Flesh*, 74. See also Peter Althouse, "Waxing and Waning of Social Deprivation as a Model for Understanding the Class Composition of Early American Pentecostalism: A Theological Assessment," in *A Liberating Spirit: Pentecostals and Social Action in North America*, eds. Michael Wilkinson and Steven Studebaker (Eugene: Pickwick Publications, 2010).

28. Yong, *Renewing Christian Theology*, 96.

132   *Chapter 6*

29. Yong, *Renewing Christian Theology*, 96.

30. Cheryl Bridges Johns, *Pentecostal Formation: A Pedagogy among the Oppressed* (Sheffield: Sheffield Academic Press, 1993), 63. For other takes on pentecostal distinctives, see: Donald W. Dayton and Robert K. Johnson, *The Variety of American Evangelicalism* (Knoxville: The University of Tennessee Press, 1991), 40–1; David Martin, *Pentecostalism: The World their Parish* (Hoboken, NJ: Wiley-Blackwell, 2001), 1; Christopher Stephenson, *Types of Pentecostal Theology*, 3ff.; Grant Wacker, *Heaven Below: Early Pentecostals and American Culture* (Boston: Harvard University Press, 2001), 30.

31. Of what we know, Bartleman wrote 550 articles, 100 tracts, 6 books, and 2 long pamphlets. See Frank Bartleman, *Witness to Pentecost: The Life of Frank Bartleman* (New York and London: Garland Publishing, Inc., 1985), viii.

32. See Augustus Cerillo Jr., "Frank Bartleman: Pentecostal 'Lone Ranger' and Social Critic," in *Portraits of a Generation: Early Pentecostal Leaders*, eds. James R. Goff Jr. and Grant Wacker (Fayetteville: The University of Arkansas Press, 2002), 105–22.

33. Frank Bartleman, "Present Day Conditions," *Weekly Evangel* 93 (June 5, 1915): 3. See also Jay Beaman, *Pentecostal Pacifism: The Origin, Development, and Rejection of Pacific Belief among the Pentecostals* (Eugene: Wipf and Stock, 1989), 76; Bartleman, *Witness to Pentecost,* xi. As Cecil Robeck, Jr. writes, "this tract was judged by E. N. Bell, manager of the Assemblies of God Publishing House, to be 'entirely too radical for war times and might even be understood in such times as pro-German and against our Allies', it was also available in tract form from the Assemblies of God." Bartleman, *Witness to Pentecost*, xi.

34. Frank Bartleman, "The Money God," *Word and Work* (circa 1916/1917): 374–5.

35. See Frank Bartleman referenced in David Wilkerson, *A Christless Pentecost: Is Christ Becoming a Stranger in Our Midst?* (Pretty Good Printing, 1982).

36. Bartleman, "Last Day Facts," *Maran-atha* 6:8–9 (May–June 1930): 8.

37. Frank Bartleman, "Christian Citizenship," Tract (located by the Flower Pentecostal Heritage Center archive).

38. Bartleman, "Last Day Facts," 8–9.

39. Mike Davis, "Planet of the Slums: Urban Involution and the Informal Proletariat," *New Left Review* 26 (March–April 2004): 31.

40. The impetus of this critique comes from Murray Dempster on the loss of pentecostal pacifism and adoption of militarism. I, however, am using it in the parallel issue of anti-capitalism and capitalism. Murray Dempster, "'Crossing Borders': Arguments Used by Early American Pentecostals in Support of the Global Character of Pacifism," *The Journal of the European Pentecostal Theological Association* X:II (1991): 75–6.

41. See Margaret Poloma's engagement with the Weberian theses of charisma and routinization in Margaret Poloma, *The Charismatic Movement: Is There a New Pentecost?* (Boston: Twayne, 1982) and *The Assemblies of God at the Crossroads: Charisma and Institutional Dilemmas* (Knoxville: University of Tennessee Press, 1989). Amos Yong offers a pointed summary of Poloma's findings, which bolsters the claim here that Pentecostals started losing their (sociopolitical) prophetic identity

and power by way of socioeconomic ascension and political conformism. Yong, *The Spirit of Creation*, 55.

42. Hollenweger, *Pentecostalism*, 186.

43. See William Faupel, *The Everlasting Gospel: Significance of Eschatology in the Development of Pentecostal Thought* (Blandford Forum: Deo Publishing, 2008), 54.

44. James K. A. Smith, *Thinking in Tongues: Pentecostal Contributions to Christian Philosophy* (Grand Rapids: William B. Eerdmans Publishing Company, 2010), 12.

45. Yong, *The Spirit Poured Out on All Flesh*, 136.

46. Frank Bartleman, "Power in a Pentecostal Congregation" in *The Company of Preachers: Wisdom on Preaching, Augustine to the Present*, ed. Richard Lischer (Grand Rapids: William B. Eerdmans Publishing Company, 2002): 421.

47. Frank Bartleman, "Power in a Pentecostal Congregation," 419–20.

48. Hence, one of the early accounts of anti-intellectualism that continues to inhibit the development of a critical Pentecostal theology is the love-hate relationship with the body.

49. See Yong, *Discerning the Spirit(s)*, 172.

50. Haynes, *Immanent Transcendence*, 1.

51. Hollenweger, *Pentecostalism*, 218.

52. Hollenweger, *Pentecostalism*, 218.

53. Smith, *Thinking in Tongues*, 42.

54. Yong, *Discerning the Spirit(s)*, 173.

55. For example, Dario Lopes Rodriguez, "The God of Life and the Spirit of Life: The Social and Political Dimension of Life in the Spirit," *Studies in World Christianity* 17:1 (2011): 1–11; Murray Dempster, "Evangelism, Social Concern, and the Kingdom of God," in *Called and Empowered: Global Mission in Pentecostal Perspective*, eds. Murray A. Dempster, Byron D. Klaus, Douglas Petersen (Peabody, MA: Hendrickson Publishers, 1991), 22–43; Johns, *Pentecostal Formation*; Hollenweger, *Pentecostalism;* Donald Miller, "2006 SSSR Presidential Address—Progressive Pentecostals: The New Face of Christian Social Engagement," *Journal for the Scientific Study of Religion* 46:4 (2007): 435–45; Donald Miller and Tetsunao Yamamori, eds. *Global Pentecostalism: The New Face of Christian Social Engagement* (Berkeley, Los Angeles, and London: University of California Press, 2007).

56. Alain Badiou, *Philosophy for Militants* (London: Verso, 2012), 27.

57. Therein resides the postsecular critique of neoliberal politics and liberal, progressive theologies.

58. Yong, *Discerning the Spirit(s)*, 100. See also Yong, *Discerning the Spirit(s)*, 102n6.

59. Yong, *Discerning the Spirit(s)*, 103; Yong, *Beyond the Impasse*, 64–5; Yong, *The Spirit Poured Out on All Flesh*, 156; Yong, *The Dialogical Spirit*, 3; Yong, "On Divine Presence and Divine Agency," 174.

60. Yong, *Discerning the Spirit(s)*, 103. In short, a dialectical "shifting foundationalism . . . recognizes all truth claims as historically embedded without having to locate their ground on any one undeniable foundation." Yong, *The Spirit Poured Out On All Flesh*, 156.

Bibliography

Adams, Nicholas. *Eclipse of Grace: Divine and Human Action in Hegel*. Hoboken, NJ: Wiley-Blackwell, 2013.

Althouse, Peter. "Waxing and Waning of Social Deprivation as a Model for Understanding the Class Composition of Early American Pentecostalism: A Theological Assessment." In *A Liberating Spirit: Pentecostals and Social Action in North America*, edited by Michael Wilkinson and Steven Studebaker, 113–5. Eugene: Pickwick Publications, 2010.

Altizer, Thomas. *The Gospel of Christian Atheism*. Philadelphia: The Westminster Press, 1966.

Anderson, Pamela Sue. *Ricoeur and Kant: Philosophy of the Will*. Atlanta: Scholars Press, 1993.

Badiou, Alain. "Metaphysics and the Critique of Metaphysics," *Pli* 10 (2000): 174–90.

———. *Philosophy for Militants*. London: Verso, 2012.

———. *The Rational Kernel of the Hegelian Dialectic*. Edited and translated by Tzuchien Tho. Melbourne: Re-press, 2011.

Bakunin, Michael. *Bakunin on Anarchy: Selected Works by the Activist-Founder of World Anarchism*. Edited and translated by Sam Dolgoff. New York: Vintage Books, 1971.

Bartleman, Frank. "Christian Citizenship." Tract. Located by the Flower Pentecostal Heritage Center archive.

———. "Last Day Facts." *Maran-atha* 6:8–9 (May–June 1930).

———. "The Money God." *Word and Work* (circa 1916/1917): 374–375.

———. "Power in a Pentecostal Congregation." In *The Company of Preachers: Wisdom on Preaching, Augustine to the Present*, edited by Richard Lischer, 417–22. Grand Rapids: William B. Eerdmans Publishing Company, 2002.

———. "Present Day Conditions." *Weekly Evangel* 93 (June 5, 1915): 3

———. *Witness to Pentecost: The Life of Frank Bartleman*. New York and London: Garland Publishing, Inc, 1985.

136 *Bibliography*

Beaman, Jay. *Pentecostal Pacifism: The Origin, Development, and Rejection of Pacific Belief among the Pentecostals.* Eugene: Wipf and Stock, 1989.

Berdyaev, Nicolas. "Introduction." In *Six Theosophic Points and Other Writings,* edited by Jacob Boehme, v–xxxvii. Ann Arbor, MI: University of Michigan Press, 1958.

Bridges Johns, Cheryl. *Pentecostal Formation: A Pedagogy among the Oppressed.* Sheffield: Sheffield Academic Press, 1993.

Butler, Rex. *Slavoj Žižek: Live Theory.* New York and London: Continuum, 2005.

Caputo, John. *On Religion.* London and New York: Routledge, 2001.

Caputo, John, and Michael Scanlon, eds. *Transcendence and Beyond: A Postmodern Inquiry.* Bloomington and Indianapolis: Indiana University Press, 2007.

Carew, Joseph. *Ontological Catastrophe: Žižek and the Paradoxical Metaphysics of German Idealism.* Ann Arbor, MI: Open Humanities Press, 2014.

Cerillo, Jr., August, "Frank Bartleman: Pentecostal 'Lone Ranger' and Social Critic." In *Portraits of a Generation: Early Pentecostal Leaders,* edited by James R. Goff, Jr. and Grant Wacker, 105–22. Fayetteville: The University of Arkansas Press, 2002.

Cole, Andrew. *The Birth of Theory.* Chicago and London: The University of Chicago Press, 2014.

Crockett, Clayton, and Creston Davis. "Risking Hegel: A New Reading for the Twenty-first Century." In *Hegel and the Infinite: Religion, Politics, and Dialectic,* eds. Slavoj Žižek, Clayton Crockett, and Creston Davis, 1–18. New York: Columbia University Press, 2011.

Davis, Mike. "Planet of the Slums: Urban Involution and the Informal Proletariat." *New Left Review* 26 (March–April 2004): 5–34.

Dayton, Donald, and Robert K. Johnson. *The Variety of American Evangelicalism.* Knoxville: The University of Tennessee Press, 1991.

Dempster, Murray. "'Crossing Borders': Arguments Used By Early American Pentecostals in Support of the Global Character of Pacifism." *The Journal of the European Pentecostal Theological Association* X:II (1991): 62–80.

———. "Evangelism, Social Concern, and the Kingdom of God." In *Called and Empowered: Global Mission in Pentecostal Perspective,* edited by Murray A. Dempster, Byron D. Klaus, Douglas Petersen, 22–43. Peabody, MA: Hendrickson Publishers, 1991.

Douglas, Andrew. *In the Spirit of Critique: Thinking Politically in the Dialectical Tradition.* New York: State University of New York Press, 2013.

Estrada, Ernesto. *The Structure of Complex Networks: Theory and Applications.* Oxford: Oxford University Press, 2011.

Faupel, William. *The Everlasting Gospel: Significance of Eschatology in the Development of Pentecostal Thought.* Blandford Forum: Deo Publishing, 2008.

Findlay, J. N. *Hegel: A Re-Examination.* New York: Humanities Press, 1964.

Finn, Douglas. *Life in the Spirit: Trinitarian Grammar and Pneumatic Community in Hegel and Augustine.* Notre Dame: University of Notre Dame Press, 2016.

Gelpi, Donald. "Review of *Discerning the Spirit(s): A Pentecostal-Charismatic Contribution to Christian Theology of Religions,* by Amos Yong." *Pneuma: The Journal of the Society for Pentecostal Studies* 24 (2002): 98–101.

Bibliography

Hahn, Sungsuk Susan. *Contradiction in Motion: Hegel's Organic Concept of Life and Value.* Ithaca and London: Cornell University Press, 2007.

Hamza, Agon. "Going to One's Ground: Žižek's Dialectical Materialism." In *Slavoj Žižek and Dialectical Materialism*, edited by Agon Hamza and Frank Ruda, 163–75. New York Palgrave Macmillan, 2016.

Haynes, Patrice. *Immanent Transcendence: Reconfiguring Materialism in Continental Philosophy.* London and New York: Bloomsbury Academic, 2012.

Hegel, G. W. F. *Elements of the Philosophy of Right*, translated by H. B. Nisbet. Cambridge: Cambridge University Press, 2003.

———. *The Encyclopaedia Logic (with the Zusätze): Part I of the Encyclopaedia of Philosophical Sciences*, translated by T. F. Geraets, W. A. Suchting, and H. S. Harris. Indianapolis and Cambridge: Hackett Publishing Company, Inc., 1991.

———. *The Encyclopedia of the Philosophical Sciences: The First Part of the Encyclopedia of the Philosophical Sciences in Outline.* Oxford: Oxford University Press, 1950.

———. *Hegel: The Letters*, translated by Clark Butler and Christine Seiler. Bloomington: Indiana University Press, 1984.

———. *Lectures on the Philosophy of Religion: One Volume Edition. The Lectures of 1827.* Edited by Peter C. Hodgson, translated by R. F. Brown, P. C. Hodgson, and J. M. Stewart. Berkeley, CA: University of California Press, 1988.

———. *Phenomenology of Spirit*, translated by A. V. Miller. Oxford: Oxford University Press, 1977.

———. "Reason and Religious Truth." In *Die Religion im inneren Verhaltnisse zur Wissenschaft* (1822), H. Fr. W. Hinrichs. Quoted in Beyond Epistemology, edited by Frederick Weiss, translated by A. V. Miller, 221–44. The Hague: Martinus Nijhoff, 1974.

———. *Science of Logic*, translated by George Di Giovanni. Cambridge: Cambridge University Press, 2010.

Hodgson, Peter. *Hegel & Christianity: A Reading of the Lectures on the Philosophy of Religion.* Oxford: Oxford University Press, 2005.

Hollenweger, Walter. *Pentecostalism: Origins and Developments Worldwide.* Peabody, MA: Hendrickson Publishers, 1997.

Houlgate, Stephen. "Essence, Reflexion, and Immediacy in Hegel's Science of Logic." In *A Companion to Hegel,* edited by Stephen Houlgate and Michael Bauer, 139–58. Hoboken, NJ: Wiley-Blackwell, 2011.

———. "Hegel, Desmond, and the Problem of God's Transcendence." *The Owl of Minerva* 36:2 (Spring/Summer 2005): 131–52.

———. "Substance, Causality, and the Question of Method in Hegel's Science of Logic." In *The Reception of Kant's Critical Philosophy: Fichte, Schelling, and Hegel*, edited by Sally Sedgwick, 232–52. Cambridge: Cambridge University Press, 2000.

Irenaeus, *Against the Heresies.* New York: Paulist Press, 1992/2012.

Jackson, M. W. "Hegel: The Real and the Rational." In *The Hegel Myths and Legends*, edited by Jon Stewart, 19–25. Evanston: Northwestern University Press, 1996.

138   *Bibliography*

Jameson, Frederic. *The Hegel Variations: On the Phenomenology of Spirit*. London and New York: Verso, 2010.

———. *Valences of the Dialectic*. London and New York: Verso, 2009.

Jaspers, Karl. *The Origin and Goal of History*. New Haven: Yale University Press, 1953.

Johnston, Adrian. *Žižek's Ontology: A Transcendental Materialist Theory of Subjectivity*. Chicago: Northwestern University Press, 2008.

Kearney, Richard. *On Paul Ricoeur: The Owl of Minerva*. Burlington, VT: Ashgate, 2004.

Kotsko, Adam. *Žižek and Theology*. New York: T & T Clark, 2008.

Krummel, John and Shigenori Nagatomo. *Place and Dialectic: Two Essays by Nishida Kitarō*. Oxford: Oxford University Press, 2012.

Lack, Tony. "Review Essay: Slavoj Žižek: Absolute Trouble or Recoil in Paradise?" *Logos* 15:2–3 (Summer 2016). http://logosjournal.com/2015/lack-Žižek-review/.

Malabou, Catherine. *The Future of Hegel: Plasticity, Temporality and Dialectic*. London and New York: Routledge, 2005.

Martin, David. *Pentecostalism: The World their Parish*. Hoboken, NJ: Wiley-Blackwell, 2001.

McGowan, Todd. "Hegel in Love." In *Can Philosophy Love? Reflections and Encounters*, edited by Cindy Zeiher and Todd McGowan, 3–26. London and New York: Rowman and Littlefield, 2017.

———. "The Necessity of an Absolute Misunderstanding: Why Hegel Has So Many Misreaders." In *Slavoj Žižek and Dialectical Materialism*, edited by Agon Hamza and Frank Ruda, 43–56. London: Palgrave Macmillan, 2016.

Milbank, John. "The Second Difference: For a Trinitarianism Without Reserve," *Modern Theology* 2:3 (1986): 213–4.

Miller, Donald. "2006 SSSR Presidential Address—Progressive Pentecostals: The New Face of Christian Social Engagement." *Journal for the Scientific Study of Religion* 46:4 (2007): 435–45.

Miller, Donald, and Tetsunao, eds. *Global Pentecostalism: The New Face of Christian Social Engagement*. Berkeley, Los Angeles and London: University of California Press, 2007.

Mueller, Gustav. "The Hegel Legend of 'Thesis-Antithesis-Synthesis.'" *Journal of the History of Ideas* 19:3 (June 1958): 411–14.

Nancy, Jean-Luc. *Hegel: The Restlessness of the Negative*. Minneapolis: University of Minnesota Press, 2002.

Neville, Robert Cummings. *Ultimates: Philosophical Theology*, vol. 1. New York: State University of New York Press, 2013.

O'Regan, Cyril. *The Heterodox Hegel*. New York: SUNY Press, 1994.

Oliverio, L. William. "An Interpretive Review Essay on Amos Yong's *Spirit-Word-Community: Theological Hermeneutics in Trinitarian Perspective*." *Journal of Pentecostal Theology* 18 (2009): 301–11.

———. "The One and the Many: Amos Yong and the Pluralism and Dissolution of Later Modernity." In *The Theology of Amos Yong and the New Face of Pentecostal*

Bibliography

Scholarship: Passion for the Spirit, edited by Martin Mittelstadt and Wolfgang Vondey, 45–61. London and Boston: Brill, 2013.

———. *Theological Hermeneutics in the Classical Pentecostal Tradition: A Typological Account*. Leiden and Boston: Brill, 2012

Pannenberg, Wolfhart. *Basic Questions in Theology*, vol. 2. Philadelphia: Fortress Press, 1971.

Poloma, Margaret. *The Assemblies of God at the Crossroads: Charisma and Institutional Dilemmas*. Knoxville: University of Tennessee Press, 1989.

———. *The Charismatic Movement: Is There a New Pentecost?* Boston: Twayne, 1982.

Ricoeur, Paul. *Freud and Philosophy: An Essay on Interpretation*. New Haven and London: Yale University Press, 1970.

———. "Religion, Atheism, and Faith." In *The Conflict of Interpretations: Essays in Hermeneutics*, edited by Don Ihde, 440–67. Evanston: Northwestern University Press, 1974.

Rodriguez, Dario Lopes. "The God of Life and the Spirit of Life: The Social and Political Dimension of Life in the Spirit." *Studies in World Christianity* 17:1 (2011): 1–11.

Ruda, Frank. "Hegel, Resistance, and Release." Lecture, University College Dublin, Dublin, Ireland, 2014. https://www.youtube.com/watch?v=VzTvFaDpTCY.

Schlitt, Dale. *Hegel's Trinitarian Claim: A Critical Reflection*. Leiden and Boston: Brill, 1984.

Scott-Baumann, Allison. *Ricoeur and the Negation of Happiness*. New York: Bloomsbury, 2013.

Shults, LeRon. *Reforming the Doctrine of God*. Grand Rapids, MI: William B. Eerdmans Publishing Company, 2005.

———. "Spirit and Spirituality: Philosophical Trends in Late Modern Pneumatology." *Pneuma* 30 (2008): 271–87.

Smith, James. *Thinking in Tongues: Pentecostal Contributions to Christian Philosophy*. Grand Rapids: William B. Eerdmans Publishing Company, 2010.

Stephenson, Christopher. "Pentecostal Theology According to the Theologians: An Introduction to the Theological Methods of Pentecostal Systematic Theologians." PhD diss. Marquette University, 2009.

———. "Reality, Knowledge, and Life in Community: Metaphysics, Epistemology, and Hermeneutics in the Work of Amos Yong." In *The Theology of Amos Yong and the New Face of Pentecostal Scholarship: Passion for the Spirit*, eds. Wolfgang Vondey and Martin Mittelstadt, 63–82. Leiden; Boston: Brill, 2013.

———. *Types of Pentecostal Theology: Method, System, Spirit*. Oxford: Oxford University Press, 2013.

Stiver, Dan. *Ricoeur and Theology*. New York: Bloomsbury, 2012.

Studebaker, Steven. "Toward a Pneumatological Trinitarian Theology: Amos Yong, the Spirit, and the Trinity." In *The Theology of Amos Yong and the New Face of Pentecostal Scholarship: Passion for the Spirit*, edited by Wolfgang Vondey and Martin Mittelstadt, 83–102. Leiden and Boston: Brill, 2013.

Taylor, Mark C. *After God*. Chicago: University of Chicago Press, 2007.

Bibliography

————. "Infinite Restlessness." In *Hegel and the Infinite: Religion, Politics, and Dialectic*, edited by Slavoj Žižek, Clayton Crockett, and Creston Davis, 91–114. New York: Columbia University Press, 2011.

————. *Journeys to Selfhood: Hegel & Kierkegaard*. Berkeley: University of California Press, 1980.

Tillich, Paul. *Systematic Theology*, vol. 1. Chicago: University of Chicago Press, 1973.

————. *Systematic Theology: Existence and the Christ*, vol. 2. Chicago: University of Chicago Press, 1975.

Vasquez, Manuel. "Studying Religion in Motion." *Method and Theory in the Study of Religion* 20 (2008): 151–84.

Verene, Donald Phillip. *Hegel's Absolute: An Introduction to Reading the Phenomenology of Spirit*. New York: State University of New York Press, 2007.

Wacker, Grant. *Heaven Below: Early Pentecostals and American Culture*. Boston: Harvard university Press, 2001.

Wilkerson, David. *A Christless Pentecost: Is Christ Becoming a Stranger in Our Midst?* Pretty Good Printing, 1982.

Williams, Robert. *Recognition: Fichte and Hegel on the Other*. New York: State University of New York Press, 1992.

Wood, Kelsey. *Žižek: A Reader's Guide*. Hoboken, NJ: Wiley-Blackwell, 2012.

Yong, Amos. *Beyond the Impasse: Toward a Pneumatological Theology of Religions*. Grand Rapids: Baker Academic, 2003.

————. *The Cosmic Breath: Spirit and Nature in the Christianity-Buddhism-Science Trialogue*. Leiden and Boston: Brill, 2012.

————. "The Demise of Foundationalism and the Retention of Truth: What Evangelicals Can Learn from C. S. Peirce," *Christian Scholar's Review* 29:3 (Spring 2000): 563–88.

————. *The Dialogical Spirit: Christian Reason and Theological Method in the Third Millennium*. Eugene, OR: Cascade Books, 2014.

————. *Discerning the Spirit(s): A Pentecostal-Charismatic Contribution to Christian Theology of Religions*. Sheffield: Sheffield Academic Press, 2000.

————. "Discerning the Spirit(s) in the World of Religions: Toward a Pneumatological Theology of Religions." In *No Other Gods before Me? Evangelicals and the Challenge of World Religions*, edited by John G. Stackhouse, 37–61. Grand Rapids, MI: Baker Academic, 2001.

————. *In the Days of Caesar: Pentecostalism and Political Theology*. Grand Rapids: W. B. Eerdmans, 2010.

————. "Not Knowing Where the Spirit Blows...': On Envisioning a Pentecostal-Charismatic Theology of Religions." *Journal of Pentecostal Theology* 14 (April 1999): 81–112.

————. "On Divine Presence and Divine Agency: Toward a Foundational Pneumatology," *Asian Journal of Pentecostal Studies* (July 2000): 167–88.

————. "Oneness and the Trinity: The Theological and Ecumenical Implications of 'Creation Ex Nihilo' for an Intra-Pentecostal Dispute," *PNEUMA* 19:1 (Spring 1997): 81–107.

———. "Possibility and Actuality: The Doctrine of Creation and Its Implications for Divine Omniscience." *The Wesleyan Philosophical Society Online Journal* 1:1 (2001). http://home.snu.edu/~brint/wpsjnl/Yong01.htm.

———. *Renewing Christian Theology: Systematics for a Global Christianity*. Waco: Baylor University Press, 2014.

———. "Review of *Exclusion and Embrace: A Theological Exploration of Identity, Otherness and Reconciliation* and *After Our Likeness: The Church as the Image of the Trinity*." *Wesleyan Theological Journal* 33:2 (1998): 259–63.

———. *The Spirit of Creation: Modern Science and Divine Action in the Pentecostal-Charismatic Imagination*. Grand Rapids: W. B. Eerdmans, 2011.

———. *Spirit of Love: A Trinitarian Theology of Grace*. Waco: Baylor University Press, 2012.

———. *The Spirit Poured Out on All Flesh: Pentecostalism and the Possibility of Global Theology*. Grand Rapids: Baker Academic, 2005.

———. *Spirit-Word-Community: Theological Hermeneutics in Trinitarian Perspective*. Burlington, VA: Ashgate, 2002.

———. *Theology and Down Syndrome: Reimagining Disability in Late Modernity*. Waco, TX: Baylor University Press. 2007.

———. "A Theology of the Third Article? Hegel and the Contemporary Enterprise in First Philosophy and First Theology." In *Semper Reformandum: Studies in Honour of Clark H. Pinnock*, edited by Stanley E. Porter and Anthony R. Cross, 208–31. Carlisle: Paternoster Press, 2003.

———. "Tongues of Fire in the Pentecostal Imagination: The Truth of Glossolalia in Light of R. C. Neville's Theory of Religious Symbolism." *Journal of Pentecostal Theology* 12 (April 1998): 39–65.

———. "The Turn to Pneumatology in Christian Theology of Religions: Conduit or Detour?" *Journal of Ecumenical Studies* 35:3–4 (1998): 437–54.

———. "Whither Systematic Theology? A Systematician Chimes in on a Scandalous Conversation." *Pneuma: The Journal of the Society for Pentecostal Studies* 20:1 (Spring 1998): 85–93.

Žižek, Slavoj. *Absolute Recoil: Towards a New Foundation of Dialectical Materialism*. London and New York: Verso, 2014.

———. "Christianity Against the Sacred." In *God in Pain: Inversions of Apocalypse*, edited by Slavoj Žižek and Boris Gunjević, 43–72. New York: Seven Stories Press, 2012.

———. "Concluding Roundtable: St. Paul among the Historians and the Systematizers." In *St. Paul among the Philosophers*, edited by John Caputo and Linda Alcoff, 160–83. Bloomington: Indiana University Press, 2009.

———. "The Descent of Transcendence into Immanence or, Deleuze as a Hegelian." In *Transcendence: Philosophy, Literature, and Theology Approach the Beyond*, edited by Regina Schwartz, 235–48. New York and London: Routledge, 2004.

———. "Dialectical Clarity versus the Misty Conceit of Paradox." In *The Monstrosity of Christ: Paradox or Dialectic?* edited by Creston Davis, 234–306. Cambridge, MA and London: The MIT Press, 2009.

142 *Bibliography*

———. *Did Somebody Say Totalitarianism? Five Interventions in the (Mis)use of a Notion.* London and New York: Verso, 2001.

———. "The Fear of Four Words: A Modest Plea for the Hegelian Reading of Christianity." In *The Monstrosity of Christ: Paradox or Dialectic?*, edited by Creston Davis, 24–109. Cambridge, MA and London: The MIT Press, 2009.

———. *For They Know Not What They Do: Enjoyment as a Political Factor.* London and New York: Verso, 1991/2008.

———. *The Fragile Absolute or, Why Is the Christian Legacy Worth Fighting For?* London: Verso Press, 2000.

———. "Hegel and Shitting: The Idea's Constipation." In *Hegel and the Infinite: Religion, Politics, and Dialectic,* edited by Slavoj Žižek, Clayton Crockett, and Creston Davis, 221–32. New York: Columbia University Press, 2011.

———. *The Indivisible Remainder.* London and New York: Verso, 1996.

———. *Interrogating the Real.* Edited by Rex Butler and Scott Stephens. London and New York: Bloomsbury Academic, 2005.

———. "Is God Dead, Unconscious, Evil, Impotent, Stupid . . . Or Just Counterfactual?" *International Journal of Žižek Studies* 10:1 (2016): 1–31.

———. "Is it Still Possible to be a Hegelian Today?" In *The Speculative Turn: Continental Materialism and Realism*, edited by Levi Bryant, Nick Srnicek, and Graham Harman, 202–23. Melbourne: Re.press, 2011.

———. *Less Than Nothing: Hegel and the Shadow of Dialectical Materialism.* London: Verso Press, 2012.

———. *Metastases of Enjoyment: Six Essays on Woman and Causality.* London and New York: Verso, 1994.

———. *The Most Sublime Hysteric: Hegel with Lacan.* Translated by Thomas Scott-Railton Cambridge and Malden, MA: Polity, 2014.

———. *On Belief.* London and New York: Routledge, 2001.

———. "Only a Suffering God Can Save Us." In *God in Pain: Inversions of Apocalypse*, edited by Slavoj Žižek and Boris Gunjević, 155–92. New York: Seven Stories Press, 2012.

———. *Organs without Bodies: Deleuze and Consequences.* New York: Routledge, 2004.

———. *The Parallax View.* Cambridge; London: The MIT Press, 2006.

———. *The Puppet and the Dwarf: The Perverse Core of Christianity.* Cambridge and London: The MIT Press, 2003.

———. "Some Thoughts on Divine Ex-sistence." *Crisis & Critique* 2:1 (2015): 12–34.

———. *The Sublime Object of Ideology.* London and New York: Verso Press, 1989/2009.

———. *Tarrying with the Negative: Kant, Hegel, and the Critique of Ideology.* Durham: Duke University Press, 1993.

———. *The Ticklish Subject: The Absent Centre of Political Ontology.* London and New York: Verso Press, 1999.

———. *The Žižek Reader.* Edited by Elizabeth Wright and Edmond Wright. Oxford and Malden, MA: Blackwell Publishers, 1999.

Index

absence, 55, 65, 88, 92
action: divine, 22, 38, 40–46, 83, 107, 120
Adams, Nicholas, 23, 33n59, 77n75, 114n23
atheism, 28
Augustine, 18, 20, 43

Badiou, Alain, 3, 129
Bartleman, Frank, 124–26
becoming, 9, 24, 55, 64, 84, 86, 89, 94n23, 111, 119, 121–22; of God, 27, 34n75, 98, 103, 112–13; ontology of, 4, 14n42, 27, 43, 65, 87, 102, 105
Bridges Johns, Cheryl, 124

Caputo, John, 93n1, 113n2
Carew, Joseph, 10n1
Cartesian, 4–5, 42
causation, 8, 14n49, 46, 57, 86, 112, 116n54
certainty, 12n20, 14n50, 88, 102
Clayton, Philip, 45
co-creation, 21, 22, 44, 53n100
coherence, 57, 83
community, 29n22, 31n39, 50n59, 59, 61, 86, 89, 110–11, 129

complexity, 8, 9, 12n20, 19, 26, 42, 50n59, 69–70, 83, 120–21, 130n12
contextualization, 23, 39
contradiction, 24, 61–63, 68–69, 72, 77n68, 105, 116n42
creation, 7, 8, 21–22, 39, 41, 44, 46, 112–13, 126

dialectic, 2, 7, 11n11, 20, 24–27, 31n40, 42, 98; speculative, 3, 10n3, 23, 55–59, 65, 69, 71–73, 92, 95n49, 104–9, 123; trinitarian, 98
dialogue, 28n3; constructive, 23; interreligious, 17, 120
dualism, 4–6, 18, 38, 56–64, 81, 102, 110, 121, 127; metaphysical, 30n27, 38, 93n1, 99; substance, 22, 39, 74n12, 83
dynamism, 2, 8, 10, 23, 26, 40, 59, 100, 106, 121

embodiment, 9–10, 88, 122–23, 126, 128
epistemology, 18, 28, 42, 46; as ontology, 55, 64, 89, 105, 111
eschatology, 21, 45, 109, 120, 125
experience, 17, 21, 27, 32n68, 38–39, 41, 47n7, 55, 63, 84, 103, 109–11, 126–27

144 *Index*

filioque, 29n13
Findlay, J. N., 23, 24, 108, 115n33, 115n35
finite-infinite, 25, 61, 75n30, 108, 111, 128
finitude, 2, 3, 22, 57–64, 82, 87, 102–5, 108, 110, 113, 128
Finn, Douglas, 34n75

Greene, Brian, 131n20

Hodgson, Peter, 34n71, 34n72, 95n52, 117n70
Hollenweger, Walter, 13n40, 17, 28n5, 116n42, 116n45, 125, 127
Houlgate, Stephen, 15n53, 56, 73n4, 77n68

imagination: pneumatological, 8, 19–20, 37, 40, 44, 47; transcendental, 63, 65
immanence, 6, 21, 25, 38, 57, 62, 81–83, 92, 94n18, 98, 107, 121, 127
Irenaeus, 18

Jameson, Frederic, 2, 11n11, 74n18
Johnston, Adrian, 63, 76n46

Kant, Immanuel, 22, 27, 59, 63

logic, 2, 82; classical/substance, 6, 10, 60; critical/complex, 6; dialectical, 20, 33n61, 87; of essence, 61 ; incarnational, 9, 120 ; speculative, 24, 26, 64–67, 90, 103, 121; trinitarian, 10, 27, 57
love, 25, 86, 89–90, 110, 124

Malabou, Catherine, 70, 93n13
materialism: dialectical, 3, 9, 23, 87, 121, 130; reductive, 72; vulgar, 81
McGowan, Todd, 72, 105
metaphysics: classical/substance, 2, 4, 6, 10n2, 53n94, 58, 82; definition of, 2, 11n10; evolutionary, 45; Moltmann, Jürgen, 18, 52n72; Murphy, Nancy,

45; mutuality, 18, 73, 122; mystery, 7, 9, 19, 46, 92, 120; mysticism, 23, 32n55, 81, 121; semiotic, 18 ; speculative, 3, 10n1, 75n29; trinitarian, 39

Nancy, Jean-Luc, 33n61, 33n70, 68
nature, 44, 45, 102, 122; divine, 2, 52n72, 60, 109, 111; human, 89
negation, 12n13, 12n15, 25, 121; divine, 88, 110; of negation, 67, 101, 105, 106; self-, 71
negativity, 3, 24, 55–57, 62–73, 84–85, 88, 111–12, 120–24, 128; dialectical, 25, 104; speculative, 38, 98–100, 105–6
network, 4, 7, 12n20, 15n52, 25, 62, 68, 73, 81, 89, 99, 104, 109, 121, 123, 128
Neville, Robert Cummings, 19, 102
non-All, 3, 63, 73, 92, 105, 121, 122, 129

O'Regan, Cyril, 104
Oliverio, L. William, 7, 28n3

panentheism, 28, 100
Pannenberg, Wolfhart, 10n2, 14n47, 18, 29n16, 31n40, 45
pantheism, 28, 100
participation, 4, 24, 37, 45, 65; in God, 2, 20, 22, 27, 31n38, 38, 44, 89, 100, 107, 121, 128
Peacocke, Arthur, 45
Peirce, C. S., 5, 18, 44, 45
pentecostal, 17, 39, 123–30; distinctives, 28n1, 41
physics, 14n51, 36, 122
plasticity, 8, 26, 59, 65, 83, 111
Polkinghorne, John, 45
process, 4, 62, 67, 70, 84, 101, 106; developmental, 34n75; philosophy, 43; theology, 21, 28

relation: God-World, 6, 9, 25, 40, 46, 57, 60, 62, 70, 81, 89, 91, 99, 104,

110, 121, 128; mind-body, 5, 15n15, 15n56, 20, 38, 61, 63, 102, 105
resurrection, 22, 25, 45, 86, 88, 92, 110
revelation, 18, 38, 41, 62, 103, 126
Ricoeur, Paul, 11n7, 97, 115n32

Shults, F. LeRon, 14n49, 15n56, 31n40, 52n85
Smith, James K. A., 126, 127
speculative, 106
Stephenson, Christopher, 6, 7
subjectivity: complex, 9, 26, 55, 61, 70, 84, 111, 120; emerging, 2; fixed, 1, 68; inter, 2, 6, 24, 122
suffering, 26, 85, 124

Taylor, Mark C., 12n20, 14n50, 15n52, 32n58, 33n70, 74n17, 114n9
Tillich, Paul, 31n40, 74n13
transcendence, 44, 92, 100; divine, 21; dualistic, 1, 6, 8, 22, 47, 57; nondualistic, 2, 9, 38, 56, 81–87, 98, 107–9, 111
Trinity, 87, 91, 92, 101
truth, 17, 23, 24, 28, 42, 57, 64, 72, 83, 87, 91, 113, 121, 129

Whitehead, A. N., 18, 45, 52n69
Wood, Kelsey, 74n21, 75n42, 77n73

About the Author

Spencer Moffatt holds a PhD in systematic theology, taught classes on theology and religious studies, completed a clinical spiritual care residency and pediatric fellowship, and is now a hospice chaplain in Minneapolis, MN.

www.ingramcontent.com/pod-product-compliance
Ingram Content Group UK Ltd.
Pitfield, Milton Keynes, MK11 3LW, UK
UKHW010655100625
6320UKWH00002B/21